THE HERMETIC PHILOSOPHY

Volume II

Being the teachings of

I-EM-HOTEP

through

MRS. K. BARKEL

THE SCHOOL OF ESOTERIC THOUGHT

72, QUEEN'S GATE, LONDON, S.W.7

PRICE 6/- NET   POSTAGE 4d

THE   HERMETIC   PHILOSOPHY

Volume II

THIS BOOK IS DEDICATED

TO

THE PUPILS OF I-EM-HOTEP, THROUGHOUT THE WORLD

Printed in Great Britain by the ALMORRIS PRESS LTD.
3, Lansdowne Road, Holland Park, London, W.11.

PREFACE

To AVOID misconceptions that have arisen concerning the teaching contained in the books known as " The Hermetic Philosophy " and " The Dawn of Truth," we think a short account of their origins might be of interest to the readers of the present volume.

In 1935-36, a desire was expressed by the members of " White Hawk's " class of philosophy held at the Headquarters of the Marylebone Spiritualist Association, that an esoteric branch of the Association might be formed for the furtherance of the teaching given by the guides of Mrs. Barkel. To achieve this end, co-operation was effected with the President and Secretary, namely Mr. Craze and Mr. Hawken, two gentlemen who were always most sympathetic in their attitude towards anything that would further the interest of their members, and as a result of this co-operation, an esoteric section to the Marylebone Spiritualist Association was formed, consisting of about 60 members, all of whom were initiated into the first degree of the " Order of the Dawn."

With regard to the subject matter of these lectures comprising " The Dawn of Truth " and " The Hermetic Philosophy," Vol. I, and also this present volume. It should be fully understood that these three books are intended for beginners, who, having proved survival through the many excellent channels provided by the Marylebone Spiritualist Association, have expressed a wish for further teaching concerning the " Whence, Why and Whither " of the soul.

To those who desire help from these lectures, we should point out that simple language has been used, as the Guides always said that their teaching was graded to suit the mind of the simplest member present. There are, however, many doors yet to be opened, through which glimpses of the beauty of the universe and of man's ultimate destiny of perfection can be obtained.

The " Order of the Dawn " was founded in 1922 and is an inner order of the School of Esoteric Thought. Its groups are all over the world, one branch alone consisting of over 5,000 members, its teachings many and varied according to grade. These cannot of course be published : one does not give a child a razor to play with.

We do not claim to teach the erudite; this has already been done by the founders of The Golden Dawn, and the Theosophical Society. We aim at first to prove survival through ordinary methods of mediumship and psychic and mental sciences, thus leading from the gate of the temple to the innermost Shrine.

The healers trained by this School have had many miraculous cures, which can be verified. I-Em-Hotep and his healers at one time had as many as 100 patients in one evening. Proofs of the continuity of life have also been given and are incontrovertible.

Our students are trained at the present time to become teachers of the New Age and comprise statesmen, scientists, bankers and members of all grades of society. We close this preface with the prayer of the Indian Students.

London, January, 1943.   **K.B.**

PRAYER FOR RACIAL RECONCILIATION

GOD of all nations, we pray Thee for all peoples of Thy earth; for those who are consumed in mutual hatred and bitterness; for those who make bloody war upon their neighbours; for those who tyrannously oppress; for those who groan under cruelty and subjection.

We pray Thee for those who bear rule and responsibility; for child races and dying races; for outcast tribes, the backward and the downtrodden; for the ignorant, the wretched and the enslaved.

We beseech Thee to teach mankind to live together in peace, no man exploiting the weak, no man hating the strong, each race working out its own destiny unfettered, self-respecting, fearless.

Teach us to be worthy of freedom, free from social wrong, free from individual oppression and contempt, pure of heart and hand, despising none, defrauding none, giving to all men in all their dealings of life the honour we owe to those who are Thy children, whatever their race, their colour or their caste. Amen.

CONTENTS

LIGHT ON THE PATH

TO-NIGHT we enter upon a new series of talks and it is hoped that we shall get down to hard work, because I propose to outline for you the way that leads from Aspirant to Hierophant—a long road. Before we commence our work in earnest, it will be necessary to throw a little light upon the path we are going to tread, therefore to-night we will talk of many things and make many resolutions.

Many of the subjects with which we will deal have been called occult or hidden, but the time has now arrived when these things should begin to percolate into the minds of men, because world conditions demand the God-light, and we must carry the God-light.

I want you to visualize yourselves as members of the outer court of one of my own colleges in Egypt, so let us imagine in the courtyard of our college a Divine Fountain, and as aspirants on the path seeking the God-light, we take our cups to the Fountain and draw from it the living waters. We slake our thirst, and having found the source of living waters, at a later date we shall go again to the Fountain to slake the thirst of others.

You have been told that it takes three incarnations to arrive at the degree of spiritual awakening necessary to become an aspirant on the Path of

Initiation, and according to the work done in previous incarnations, some are naturally better equipped than others for the task that lies ahead. But in this day of life it is again left to the aspirant to decide whether to go forward, or to dally by the roadside.

As we tread the Path of Attainment, a re-adjustment of ideas and of modes of living will be necessary, for it is a path of constant endeavour, and the Gods do not bestow wisdom unless a soul reaches out for it. It is possible that you may have attended many lectures and heard various teachers, and these teachers may have tried to interest you, because they saw that you were ready for certain teaching. They may have told you that you are a healer, or that you will become clairvoyant or clairaudient, or even a great Teacher. They may have been quite right in making such statements, because they may have seen in you your possibilities, but remember, these Teachers have only promised rewards much in the same way as you would promise a child sweetmeats if it did certain things. It is for you, however, to fit yourselves for the task that lies ahead. Within every one of you there are potentialities of Godhead. You are all healers, seers or teachers in the making, but first you have to fit yourselves for the work, and part of your training consists of making yourselves conversant with the inhabitants and geography of the spiritual worlds.

Before you can be a Teacher, you must learn to

speak with authority, and be able to say to those you teach, "For many years I have sought the more interior way, I have learned the wisdom of the Gods, I know the pitfalls that await you, nevertheless, the things I teach and seek to interest you in, I know to be true." Until a man has experienced the truth of the spiritual realms and can be sure in his mind, he has no right to teach esoteric thought. I speak in this way that you may realize the responsibilities you are taking up if you become an aspirant in the Hermetic section of this school, because you will be drawn apart, you will come under the special guidance of a group of Teachers, and from the moment this happens, your thoughts are not your own.

Your thoughts are reviewed consciously, subconsciously, and super-consciously, by those who have taken you into their keeping. They will not listen to any excuse; but having commenced to tread the path you must go on until you learn to look into the stone of truth. You must not be afraid for your fellow students to know your weaknesses. You have to watch every word you speak, because your desire for wisdom has brought you into association with the great White Lodges of the Brotherhood of Angels and Men. You become a target for opposing forces, and those opposing forces will reach you through weaknesses of character, and destroy the most simple things of your daily life. I do not wish to depress you, but I do want you to realize how impossible it is for you to make any progress on the more interior pathway if you are not prepared to be perfectly honest with yourself and your neighbours. It is the Age-old teaching: "Do unto others as thou would have them do to you." And what can I promise you for all this? Serenity of spirit, a joyousness, a new interest in life. A realization that all your difficulties, all your ill-health, everything that comes to you, is an opportunity you may use to cleanse and purify your soul.

Already you have been taught that the Lodge of Masters is no fabrication of an imaginative mind. The Lodge of the Masters is a real and concrete organization. It has both inner and outer lodges; it has its Adepts and its Disciples, in every country of the world, and what to you may look like chaos or injustice, may be God's way of working for perfection. Therefore, an aspirant on the path must first of all learn that he is a citizen of the world, not of any special country, that he is a child of God, of no especial parents, and he is both incarnate and discarnate. When you recognize that you all have a common Parent who is God and also Father and Mother, you will then realize that you are all of one family, and that caste ceases to be. You realize that as younger or elder brothers and sisters, each do your task according to the bidding of your Divine Parents. Some of you may be doing the very menial task of cleansing the floor; others for the first time may be given charge of wealth, to see how they use it. Those who strive to do their duty carefully and well shall, in time, become inheritors of the Kingdom.

It is a great thing to remember that the aspirant on the path must have no belongings, therefore, learn to let go. Do not clutch at your possessions so much; look upon them as something lent to you to do your especial task in this day of life; and remember that when you leave the physical body the only thing that you can carry with you is that which belongs to the mind. Lay up for yourselves the treasures of heaven; let growth of character count more with you than gold; let beauty and cleanliness of body count with you also, because, for the time being, your body is a temple holding a part of God, therefore you must beautify, cleanse and guard it. As you do this, you are rewarded by good health and pure and uplifting thoughts. When you fill your mind with divine thought you have no room for criticism of your neighbour, because whatever your neighbour does, he may have been commanded to do, to test you. Remember that at some time on the path, you will have to face the result of your criticisms, your unjust remarks, your coldness and disdain, so it is your duty to strive after perfection. Those who have a little knowledge realize that there are three hundred and sixty different types of people, therefore we must endeavour to discover the faults and the virtues of those different types. For instance, in Astrology, we may have a person whose ascendant is Aries, another whose ascendant is Taurus, or maybe Scorpio; instead of classifying them sweepingly as Arians, Taureans or Scorpios, we must realize that there are thirty degrees to each sign, therefore to each sign there are thirty different types. This enables us to understand that we may react to different circumstances in different ways; when we have grasped that idea, we are able to take our first lesson in tolerance.

This first talk I have called "Light on the Path," and it may seem to you that I have shown very little of the Light, but you find that as you learn the things I strive to teach, and which you must make the effort to gain, that all the gifts of the spirit can become yours, another world opens up in front of you; the birds, as they sing, have a meaning for you; the flowers, as they bloom in their seasons, bring you a message; the wind, as it whispers through the trees, tells you of the higher planes. The Moon is your mother, and the Sun your father, because they are the outer symbols of the force which lies behind, and in the cold, pale light of the Moon, with your heart you learn to reach out and up to that Great and Divine Spirit who fostered you when first you incarnated on the earth plane, and the feeling of adoration grows. As you recognise the Divine Mother, she pours her gifts of the psychic plane into your soul, and you become her reverberator. As you image the warmth and power of the Sun, you begin to image your Father; you feel His strength permeating every particle of your being, and He brings to you remembrance of how you dwelt with Him on the plane of spirit. He brings to your remembrance how you have striven Age after Age to reach Him, and He inspires you with Divine Love. He paints in your mind glowing pictures wherewith you can retail to others the love of the Father and the wisdom of the Mother; the world loses its drabness; life takes on a deeper meaning, and you realize your freedom from the slavery of the world. You no longer feel that God has dealt with you harshly and unjustly; you recognize that your environment, your difficulties, your joys and your sorrows have been of your own making; you take up the staff that is put into the hand of every aspirant, and you stand forth boldly and commence to tread the more interior way.

What will you meet on the path? Friends who will misunderstand and misjudge you, and say hurtful things about you, and you will feel as though the world falls about your feet. And when they find that you do not retaliate, they will scandalize you. But, be steadfast, be strong in faith, because those who are wrapped in the Aura of God, cannot be harmed. Each day will bring strength, power, an awareness of companionship; never more are you alone; your Angel Teacher walks by your side and whispers words of comfort, words of cheer, and if you remember to listen to his voice, you overcome all difficulties. You are merged in the gathering of wisdom, and you learn patience. You will not be over-anxious to teach before you have knowledge or to display your gifts of seer-ship until you are sure that you are not seeing the reflections of the astral world. You will not be over-anxious to teach, before you have knowledge; but slowly, steadfastly and surely, you will unfold your gifts on each plane of consciousness, and stand forth as a herald of the Dawn in this New Age. Because in this New Age, my friends, all pretence, all dishonesty, and all that is unreal, must go. This breaking down of old conditions is brought about in order that a sure and strong foundation of truth shall be placed upon the earth, so that when the great and loving Voice of God wends His way earthward, the Church of the New Civilisation shall be founded, and it shall be founded on love, truth and unity. But before that can take place, you have to fight the forces of the black lodges; you have to face truth, and be open and free one with another. Light on the path comes; light on the path shines out strongly and clearly, when you have forgotten the self. When the eyes have become incapable of tears, when the feet have been washed in the blood of the heart. That means that when the feet are tired and there has been no reward for much work done, the heart bleeds because there is no recognition, then all of the self goes, and the feet having been washed in the blood of the heart, serve only God, and seek no recognition from anyone but God. "The eyes have become incapable of tears." What causes tears? When you are sorry that you are misunderstood; when someone you love has hurt you. When you have become incapable of self-pity, when others are unable to wound you, then your heart is filled with a Divine Love and there is no room for self-pity. You seek only to help others. Impersonality does not mean a crushing out or coldness, it means a ready sympathy and understanding for all those who are weaker or have less knowledge than yourself. It means that no one has the power to hurt you, once you have realized your unity with God; no one can harm you; no one can hurt the real self, because the spirit inside is singing its paean of praise and joining in the great and grand Hosannah. The spirit, triumphant over the smallness of the personality, can hear the harmony of the world.

Let not my words lessen your aspirations, I have only tried to make you understand some of the things you will meet. If you have the power to tread the pathway, then in time you become a ruler of all the interior worlds; the waters obey you, the earth yields its fruits for you, the wind becomes your messenger, and you become known in the elemental kingdoms as a Magian—one who has power. You attain, even as others have attained, because you are treading the way of your beloved Master Jesus; you are treading the way of all the Christed ones of all the Ages, and for you, when you have attained, is the Crown of the Initiate. You have the power to so control your mind that you can make it think and function on three planes simultaneously.   There is the super-conscious mind, where you are alive to the thought of God; there is the sub-conscious mind, and the conscious mind doing its daily tasks.   In doing your work, whether it is in the office or in the home, in the field or the road, no matter where it may be, do every-thing unto God.   Make your most simple tasks show your adoration for Him.   Let everything you do be a ritual, let every word you say be a word of power, let every thought be an anthem.   Carry the God-light with you day by day, and it shall begin to manifest through to the outer world.   As you grow in spirituality, and come into touch with your fellows, there shall be peace, love and har-mony, as sure as day follows night.

QUESTIONS

Q. I-Em-Hotep, we try our utmost to overcome our faults, and yet we stumble and fall so many times that we feel our efforts must have been feeble?

A. My daughter, it does not matter how many times a child stumbles when it is trying to walk. Each stumble or mistake teaches balance. With all your striving do not let depression take hold of you, but let each stumble make you more determined that you will overcome.   Remem-ber, you have the Mother aspect of God watch-ing you, and every Mother takes joy in watch-ing the efforts of her child to walk; her arms are ever ready to help, to hold it when the child stumbles that its hurt be not too severe, but sad would be the heart of the Mother if the child made no effort to walk. Better to make the effort and fail, then to make no effort at all. If you stumble over the same stone twice, meditate upon it, and find the weakness that made you stumble the second time and root it out; root out self-pride and self-approbation. Remember that you are the daughter of a King, and as you are the daughter of a King, remember that the greatest are filled with the most humility. If you keep that thought in your mind, it does away with pride that is easily hurt, and that is the greatest stumbling stone in the path.

Q. Are not all stumbling stones in the nature of tests to help and to purify?

A. My son, on every plane of consciousness there must of necessity be pride, and in one sense is it not human, if one has learnt control of an element, to try to show one's friends how one has progressed, but it is not lawful. I, myself, find that the more one knows of the law of the planes, the law of the stars and the law of the universe, the more one realizes how tremendous is the force that is at work and the soul stands in awe, and the lips fear to utter the little one knows.

Q. A great philosopher once said " If thou wouldst attain wisdom, be humble." We who are aspirants on the path do not always find it easy to line up to that standard.

A. My son, those who have attained wisdom are often tempted to listen to the voice of the syrens who flatter and coerce, and say " Oh, how great thou art, how much wisdom thou hast, wilt thou teach me?" And man being man, easily falls into error.

Q. I have heard it said that fear is the last tie to be overcome.

A. All problems whether of thought, ideals or ties should be brought into the open and discussed freely. Think what a joyous thing it would be if a man had nothing to hide from his fellows. He would cease to be enslaved and have banished fear, and an aspirant must have no fear. How if he has fear will he meet the difficulties on the path? If he has fear, how will be know how to distinguish the sheep from the wolf in sheep's clothing? He must learn to have clear discernment and no fear.

Q. Why is it that certain types of knowledge are difficult to acquire?

A. If you are training to be a teacher, you must have a diversity of knowledge and it is wise to persevere. For instance, suppose that you decide to study Astrology, and having learned a little about the signs and planets, and being so pleased with yourself, you cast your map and then you find it difficult to delineate. You must understand that there are much deeper things about which you must acquire knowledge, such as the fixed stars and the meanings of all the degrees. If you are drawn to Astrology, you have learned it before, if you reject it you have not learned it before and it is wise to commence.

Q. I-Em-Hotep, are not the difficulties with which we are faced simply trials on the pathway?

A. Naturally, the difficulties are trials. Suppose your teacher says '' In this incarnation it is necessary fo you to learn and practise ritual.'' You may not agree, but you obey. In spite of your dislike to go on, because your intuition tells you that you have arrived at a state of spiritual growth where ritual becomes necessary. If this happens, you will take to it like a duck to water and enjoy it, but if you are somewhat timid or dislike it, or find it difficult, then you should exercise your will power and realize you are doing it for the first time.

Q. I understand that there will come a time when there is an immediate perception of things. Of course this is a goal to which we all aspire, but it seems to me that until this time comes it is not wise to teach anything but the simplest of things because you cannot say that you know?

A. Exactly, you can say '' I believe completely and absolutely but I do not know.'' But suppose you were told to teach the simple A.B.C. to a class of young students. How would you do it? Cast your mind back to the time when you started, and remember that you had to be taught along orthodox lines, with perhaps a dash of unorthodoxy thrown in; if, however, you take those you teach along the pathway you have trod, then you can say '' These things I have learned, these things I believe, but as yet I have not received my Illumination.'' You have heard that when an aspirant reaches a certain stage on the path he receives an Illumination; that Illumination is an actual experience, and he can then say '' I know, I have seen.'' In the olden days when a student had progressed to a certain degree, he was led into the darkness beneath the temple and took what was called '' The Initiation of Death.'' He was placed in a sarcophagus, and put into a deep sleep for three days. That was his Illumination. On the third day he rose again. He had been with his Father in Heaven. And it is possible for many of you in this day of life, to go through that same Initiation, but before you can do so you have to overcome, even as the Initiates of old, because only the pure in heart can dare to face God.

Q. I take it that the opposing or black forces cannot touch a man who has eliminated pride, vanity and other faults from his nature?

A. Exactly. Only good can result from the practice of esoteric science. If the one aim in view is to cast out fear and weakness and take a firm stand, then all occultism, all esoteric science promotes the building up of the character. You cannot advance on the path if you blow hot and cold ; how can the Gods use a weapon which, when thrown, is blown about by every wind. What does it matter if you are unpopular. Slander and scandal have no effect upon the pure. If the black forces realize that you are a potent force for good, they will seek by every means in their power to undermine your growth. If you are sensitive or easily wounded, and say : '' I will not go on with this, because I am hurt,'' then the black forces can use you ; but if you throw aside the self and go straight to the one that has hurt you and say : '' We are the children of one Father. You have tried to hurt me ; what was your reason?'' The reason is given and the misunderstanding is cleared up.

Q. I-Em-Hotep, you said that we have been attracted here. Will you explain?

A. Many of you have studied these teachings in a previous incarnation, so in this day of life you are attracted to the subject of Esoteric Science, and find it interesting and easy to learn. Having been a priest in one incarnation does not mean that you have absorbed all wisdom. In my own case, when on your Earth, I earned the right to be the Hierophant of my land, but during the thousands of years I have been in the spirit land, my knowledge has been of no use. As I try to teach you, here in this room, greater knowledge is being unfolded to me, and only by helping others can I attain to more wisdom. Through this, we learn to know each other, trust each other, love each other; and when the time comes, as I hope it will, to give you your Illumination, then I shall return to my Father, and carry you as a posy of flowers, pure, white and beautiful, for the adornment of His Kingdom.

Prayer

Eternal Spirit of all good. We, Thy children, incarnate and discarnate, draw near to Thee in Spirit. We adore Thee and thank Thee, for Universal Goodness. We thank Thee Thou hast allowed us to meet together to converse for a little while, and we would ask Thee that Thou wouldst pour down upon us Thy beneficent Rays to encircle these Thy children of Earth. Join us together that we may never be parted. I, Thy servant, speak to Thee in their name, asking for them Thine infinite peace, and the glory of Thy love around them. The peace of Thy voice to guide them. Thy wisdom to illuminate them. Thy strength to enable them to go forth in Thy ways. Purify all atoms of their bodies that all pain, all sickness is made to fall away. Pour forth Thy peace upon us Oh Thou who art our Father and our most tender of Mothers that we may rest in peace within Thy arms until we meet again. Amen.

LAYING THE FOUNDATION

TO-NIGHT we are going to talk about laying the foundation. To lay the foundation of a new life, to lay the foundation whereby we make preparation for a new journey into a fresh condition or a fresh country, must of necessity mean a great deal of inward contemplation and we have many things to consider. If we lay the foundation stone strong and firm, no winds of adversity, rain or storm, can affect us, because we never swerve from our desire for spiritual attainment, or union with God.

It sometimes happens that an aspirant on the path will observe that the Gods have chosen for their mouthpiece people who seem uneducated or are lacking in wealth, manners or social prestige, and because of this the aspirant commences to analyse the Teacher, thoughts of doubt creep into his mind as to whether he can trust the teaching. Let that aspirant remember that throughout all time the Messengers of God enter this world clothed in nothing but their wisdom. The Gods choose those who have had, in some previous day of life, the experience of wealth, intellect or social position. They use only those who are of meek and lowly spirit and they fill them with the Light that illuminates mankind.

You must be careful when you find an instru-

ment or Teacher who is using his or her gifts for
the aggrandisement of the personality by means of
intellect, wealth or position, because Teachers of
this type have been decoyed from the higher path
and are being used as instruments of destruction
by the grey brothers. Those who are meek and
lowly of spirit, those who seek not the things of the
world, are the true messengers of the Illuminati.
And so, in telling you how to lay the foundations
of the spiritual life, I want you to listen carefully
to my words. When I beg of you to live in harmony and unity one with the other, I mean it in this
way : all who are here enjoy different grades of
intellect, wealth or position, some in the Army,
others in business or at home.

I want you to realise that you do not have to step
out of your environment to do the work of the
Gods, or to imbibe the wisdom of the Gods, because the Gods have created you, and placed every
one of you in an environment, wherein by living
to the highest, you can best serve. If you have
wealth and help a soul, do not feel that you ought
to be patted on the back. Those who share their
wealth, should give lovingly and freely, remembering that in a day to come, they will have to render to the Supreme Godhead an account of their
stewardship. If they have been placed in a high
social position, they will have to give an account
of their stewardship, and should they have misused that position, they return on the river of time
as a beggar. Every-thing you have has been given

to you that you might beautify it; and so, whatever you have, whatever you strive to be, whatever you have to do, with hands, mind or lips, see that you do it perfectly and to the glory of the Most High. Let each of you live up to the highest light you have, quietly scattering the seeds of truth upon fertile ground. In this way you serve the Gods.

Wisdom is given to each of you from one source. You may however, regard me as a fountain and yourselves as travellers, you thirst, you hold your cup, that it may be filled with the waters of life.

If you are going to make headway along the path you must have a wide tolerance. You have to regard yourself as a traveller, visiting strange countries, and studying the customs and the language of the people. Therefore it is wise to learn something of all types of religious beliefs. You should attend lectures upon such subjects as New Thought, Theosophy, Christian Science and so on, and you should visit Churches of different denominations. This should teach you to see aspects of God from different angles, and as you do this time after time wearing, so to speak, the other person's shoes, learning to look through his spectacles, so do you become more tolerant.

Strive to understand the minds of others, because truth is like a diamond, and you, as we watch you from the spiritual worlds, are like diamonds also. Many of you, as you catch the Rays of the Spiritual Sun, flash back your colour; you sparkle in the beauty of the Spiritual Sun. The facet that is unaware of the Spiritual Sun and does not catch the light, still has its own faint gleam, which is the spiritual light buried within it. And the spiritual light in each heart is the light that reflects the gleams as the diamond is moved.

We, who minister unto you, are not always aware of your entire personality. What seems to you a great anxiety, we see as a faint greyness in your aura. What seems to you a great joy, we see, perhaps, as a flash of rainbow light. Therefore, try to remember that as you strive to come into at-one-ment with God, so shall strength be given to you to overcome the daily pinpricks of your personality, until the personality becomes merged into the spiritual self and you are at one with your Father. Then, all power is yours; you are able to overcome and transcend matter. I know that at times you feel lonely and sick at heart. Try, when these moods come upon you, to remember that you are free. Eventually, you must attain perfection, until you have done this there is no driving force that can take you along the path of illumination but your own self. The aspirant who treads the path, must cultivate impersonality. In the sight of God you are all spokes in the wheel of eternity, and your worldly prestige, wealth and intelligence, mean nothing to Him who lent you these things; God sees that part of himself which is in your heart centre, and according to its luminosity so does He judge you.

I am an old man, so old that I have seen countless incarnations, and many civilizations rise and fall. I have companioned kings and beggars, so I know the ways of both high and low. Therefore, I understand you. Do not come seeking the waters of the spirit with the feeling in your heart that you are honouring God; but rather, view yourself as a child who comes seeking nourishment that it may grow strong in mind and able to express God. Try to see truth in all its nakedness. Avoid teachers who flatter, and remember that when you come to I-Em-Hotep, you receive the water of life without the sugar. At the present time teaching of a sugary nature is being given out under the name of spiritual guidance but which is really a drug to spiritual advancement. I show you the light on the mountain top, and I expect you to have the strength to climb until you reach it. I want you to be filled with a divine dissatisfaction, because if you are dissatisfied, the more you will seek the interior way that brings liberation. If we persevere in our search after truth, we find when uncovering the veils, that truth is really God.

Questions

Q. I-Em-Hotep, in the case of an aspirant making an error, through pride or other desires, would that error show itself as a stain upon the aura?

A. It would depend upon the error, my son. The error may be due to misunderstanding, or misplaced zeal. You must remember that the

Guardian Spirit of the aspirant does not always show the stain of the mistake in the aura; he sometimes writes it in the Book of Life. Take the case of a proud spirit, striving to serve God on the earth plane, but through pride or ignorance has fallen into error in spite of good intentions. He might have been in a psychic atmosphere, when his aura was open and if he were an earnest aspirant on the path, the Guardian Angel would not let the stain remain in the aura, but would write it in his Book of Records, so that only the Eye of God would perceive the error. If the stain had not been removed it might have been seen psychically in the aura, perhaps to the detriment of the aspirant, making him feel that he had committed a much graver sin than was really the case.

Q. What are the qualities that you would regard as being the most helpful and necessary in order to progress upon the path?

A. Every aspirant should have honesty of purpose, a desire for union with God, a desire to progress that he or she might further God's plan on earth, because the aspirant on the path who is seeking emancipation from matter, is seeking union with God and is content to work impersonally for the good of the whole. One who desires personal gain, personal power, or personal knowledge, becomes open to the influence of those who are on the left-hand path. Those who work on the right-hand path, work

impersonally for the furtherance of God's kingdom, and for union with God only. The right-
hand and left-hand paths run parallel, and the
same knowledge must be partaken of by the
aspirants of both paths until they arrive at a
certain stage. Then there comes the parting of
the ways, and one must choose deliberately,
whether he will go right or left; and if there
is self-esteem, desire for personal gain, then,
such a one is entering the zone of the left-hand
path. Those on the left-hand path cannot use
any person whose soul is set on God. In certain cases a fault of the personality can become
a playground for mischievous denizens of the
elemental kingdoms. A half-developed psychic who wants money for some personal end,
can become the prey of the lower astral entities.

Q. I suppose we aid another by sending out helpful thoughts.

A. Until you have perfected yourselves, until you
have become faultless, and are Karma free,
why should you consider yourselves strong
. enough to be able to aid another? You see,
my child, your question illustrates the senti-
mentality of mysticism. It is not constructive.
When you are pure within, when you have no
evil thoughts, when you are filled with the oneness of God, then you can draw on the source
of all power to help you, but not until you are
bathed and filled with that Holy Radiance.
The trouble in your world to-day is that every-

body is filled with good intentions! Good intentions are not strong enough. You must be filled with the Spirit of God, and you cannot be filled with the Spirit of God until you have cast out errors from your own nature. The more advanced the aspirant on the path, the more does he aspire to further advancement, because having received spiritual illumination, he is ever hungry for the light.

Q. At the present moment it would seem that we do not know how to help the world even if we would. If this is so, would it not be better to do nothing in the matter?

A. I would put it in this way my son. Let each one of you aim at perfection in your daily life, every morning offering yourself as an empty vessel to be filled with the Holy Spirit, every moment of the day consecrating unto God all your words and actions. When you think of God, you should identify yourself with God; in that way His Radiance permeates every cell of your being and you then live as God made manifest. The very fact of your doing this would make your aura vibrate with the Divine Essence, and those who come within it must feel stronger and better. It is the radiation of the great currents of God-light within, that will bring peace and happiness to the world, rather than lip service.

Q. Is it possible to obtain that perfection whilst here in the flesh?

A. Of course it is! I am not placing impossibilities before you. It is true that the perfection I have outlined is of small and steady growth. You should, however, understand that every criticism of another, if turned to the criticism of the self, produces greater harmony in the self; when this is obtained you criticise others less. Let your Higher Self illuminate your Lower Self; in this way the personality becomes gradually cleansed of its weaknesses. One must be perfect in one's self, if one would expect perfection in others.

Q. Is it right to think of the Higher Self as our Guardian Angel?

A. It is wise to think of the Higher Self, as being companioned by your Guardan Angel. I know that in your world it is sometime said that the Higher Self is God, that the Higher Self is the Guardian Angel, but the Higher Self is that part of the spirit that is not wholly incarnate in matter, and it becomes, as it were, the inner, or instinctive self, but it is not the Guardian Spirit or Angel. Beyond the Higher Self every soul has two watchers; and you can, in coming into touch with that Higher Self, become aware, or receive an illumination that will enable you to judge rightly or wrongly about certain matters that will help the personality. In the Higher Self, which can come into touch with the Cosmic Mind, is a knowledge of good and evil, and by inward contemplation you can contact this light of the Higher Self. As you build the bridge, the lower personality commits fewer errors of judgment or of conduct. I may here remind you that I have dealt with an aspect of " The Bridge " in a previous talk.

I am hoping at the conclusion of these meetings, that over the brow of each one of you will flame the twelve-pointed star, but before that can happen you must be able to see the reflection of the light in each point and you cannot see this as long as you refuse to face anything of an unpleasant nature, so I look to you all to see that your foundation stone is well and truly laid.

PRAYER

Oh Thou who art all love ! We come to Thee. Thou who art our Mother, and who receivest us as Thy little children; take us in, that we may find refreshment and nourishment from Thy chalice of wisdom.

Help us to receive, Oh holy Mother, Thy wisdom, to illuminate our souls, for we are Thy children, incarnate and discarnate, and we seek to glorify Thee. For these Thy children of earth, lend to them Thy mirror, that as they gaze within themselves they may see Thy reflections. Clothe them with Thy cloak of righteousness; help them to have Thy healing touch. Help them to have Thy sweet ministration; help them to have Thy desire for service; help them to have Thy humility.

We ask Thee, Oh Thou divine and ever living, to reveal Thyself to them, that they may, through Thy preparation, be able to stand filled with Thy wisdom, in the white light of our Father. We ask Thee to give them sweet rest and peace, that they may waken refreshed to carry out the Father's command that as they touch other children of Thine, that they will give them a little of that wisdom with which Thou hast inspired us. Now, gather us in Thy eternal peace. Amen.

PREPARATION FOR INITIATION

PREPARATION for initiation may seem to some of you rather a long title from my address to-night, but it is necessary that you learn something of the work to be done before you can become an accepted Disciple on the Path of Holiness. Many Ages have passed—I think about 5,000 years—since I trod your earth and, of necessity, times have changed. In my day, if one were going to take Initiation it was necessary to give up the whole of the life to preparation; but the Gods, as they patiently watch the struggles of humanity, ever try to meet the new conditions and so, to-day, it is only necessary that you give up part of each day. Remember, I have often told you that every step of the way entails hard work, that nothing is acquired easily; and so Initiation does not consist solely of going through a ceremony and becoming accepted into a group, church or brotherhood. It is something much deeper, and the nature of the path differs for each soul that treads it. No person can reach the goal by treading in the footsteps of one who has gone before; each soul must find its own path. The Gods, Masters and Guides, as they look on, are aware of the Chela's difficulty. For one, meditation may be hard; for another, it is easy; or perhaps for one it may be difficult to hear the inner voice, for

44

another the inner voice can be heard with ease; therefore it will be well to hold the mind in a state resembling fluidity. We have to learn that every disciple on the path has the same goal in view, but cannot tread the same path; it is also interesting to note that there are many approaches to these paths and that on the Kabalistic Tree of Life will be found the outlines of each part of these paths. With this knowledge we shall realize that the first lesson to be learned is tolerance one towards another. In a study group we often find that one will assimilate a certain line of teaching far more quickly than another. One person may find the symbols of Astrology easy to understand, another will respond more readily to the symbology of numbers, whilst yet another will see God in sound or colour.

At the beginning, it must be clearly understood that there are twelve ways by which the soul can find its way God-wards, and such ways can be by means of sound, form, number, colour, touch or sight, to enumerate some of them. As long as a soul seeks to become perfected along one particular line, it shows it is preparing for Initiation; because, in one day of life or another, it has to learn all types of thought. You cannot become what is termed an Adeptus Minor, or an Adeptus Major, until you have garnered experience during many days of life.

As we start out on our preparation for Initiation, we have to learn first and foremost that we cannot travel in company. The road of Initiation must be travelled alone, therefore the soul must be prepared for aloneness. Another lesson to be learned is adaptability; otherwise, when one student tries to teach another his method of procedure, there may be some inharmony, because the one teaching feels that he has advanced a little beyond the student he is trying to teach, and he is apt to become somewhat irritated if the one he is teaching fails to understand his point of view, or perhaps goes off into some side path that makes a greater appeal.

An advanced student can become of no use to his Guru unless his mind exhibits the quality of adaptability. Suppose you are learning the more interior way and you desire to help another soul by means of Astrology; a study of his horoscope may show that the element Earth predominates, therefore as his Teacher, you must add the element Fire in order to warm and generate force; or it may be that there are too many planets in Water signs, in which case you would find it necessary to add Fire and Air and so forth, according to each individual horoscope. No student on the pathway should begin to teach until he has learned that he must have the power to place these elements where best they will enhance the growth of the one he is trying to help. You will now understand more clearly why I have sometimes deplored that you gather together in groups for discussion, but having so little knowledge you merely add confusion to confusion, so that when one student has perhaps begun to " see," he suddenly finds that interior sight closed down; or it might be that you accept advice from a student whose Astrological tendencies are leading him along the pathway of sound, and in trying to do *his* exercises and make progress in *his* way, you close down your own avenue of reaching the goal by stamping out, shall we say, the element of Water, which gave you power to see the Creative Light.

During the time that you attend these classes, you must never feel that you are alone. The Guru has much personal interest in you as far as your growth is concerned, but in striving to make you understand that the road you must travel, must be travelled alone, He tries to convey to you the impression of impersonality. Another thing I would touch upon pertains to the egotistical chatter that goes on amongst you sometimes, when a few of you gather together. It is painful to your Higher Self, and causes your guides and Masters a great amount of trouble, as they have to disentangle from your aura the thought forces of others. Do try to remember that if you desire to tread the more interior way, you must go alone. You must never talk about your experiences in meditation or in concentration, except to your Guru. You must never express your ideas concerning, shall we say, Cosmic Forces, except to your Guru, because your Guru is able to give you the understanding and clarification necessary for your soul's growth. I once heard one Chela say to another : " When meditating on Saturn, I saw the colour green, and so Saturn and the colour green go together," to be met with the reply : " You are wrong. I am sure I saw the colour blue for Saturn." Each is seeing a different aspect of Saturn, according to the Ray and aspect of each Chela's Sun at that particular time. Both are right, but neither can grasp the truth without greater knowledge. And so it is with everything.

You are here upon the earth plane that you may gain self-individualization. Many of you have returned day after day of time to garner your experience. Some of you are only just escaping from group guidance and have a sense of fear in being alone; you feel that unless you are popular or surrounded by friends, you are not doing what the Gods would wish you to do. Let me once more emphazise that for the self-individualization of the soul it is necessary to be much alone, because in this silence and aloneness, the soul gradually becomes self-individualized, it is able to hold converse with the Father in Heaven. It is attuned to where it can receive the direct Ray of teaching necessary for its evolution; also in this aloneness, the soul becomes aware of the all-enveloping love of the Guru who, for the time being, has it in charge.

You see, then, how necessary it is for each one of you to try to cultivate within yourself a shrine, which should be in the Heart Centre, where no one should enter but your Higher Self; because, to tread the more interior way and go through your Initiations, it is necessary for you to go alone. I would mention here that there is a book entitled " The Book of the Sacred Magic," that you might do well to study. It will help you to realize the necessity for aloneness. You will be wise if you do not follow this book too literally or too closely, and do not attempt the Initiation described in it, unless guided by one who has already taken it. Apart from this it will teach you how close your Guardian Angel is to you, and make clear the nature of His tests; it will also teach you how to come into touch with the Dweller on the Threshold, and tell you how the different Guides will try to test you as they come in the guise of pride, lust, jealousy, and so on, and it will help you perhaps to realize that the more intense, the more desirous a soul is to reach to union with the Godhead, the stronger it becomes as it treads the path of aloneness.

Now do not mistake my meaning when I stress the importance of aloneness : it only applies to spiritual things. To meet together in groups and speak lightly of Initiation and the travail of the soul is unthinkable; but to gather together in friendly converse in social life is quite a different matter. The things of the spirit should be buried deep in the mind, and only brought to the surface during the time of contemplation or meditation. Make a strong line of demarcation between the two sides of you, the conscious mind and physical body:

D

living the every day life, not appearing peculiar, not seeking to be superior, or proud, or desiring to air the knowledge that you have gained through intercourse with discarnate entities; but being just a normal, healthy, ordinary type of person; leaving the side of you that reflects the Inner Life, for when you enter the silence. These periods of quietness can take place at any time, it matters not whether it is morning, noon or evening. The Conscious mind is stilled, and the Super-conscious mind blends with the Sub-conscious mind, making you a different person, because you have put away earthly things and are companioned by Angels. You are in the direct thought Ray of your Teacher, and you have come into at-one-ment with your Father in Heaven. As you spend this quiet hour in the innermost sanctuary of your heart, raising your consciousness to the higher planes, your body is rested and your nerves are stilled, and because you have learned to separate the two selves, your inner sight and hearing become familiar with the interior planes, you become aware of an inflow of force, you become conversant with the voice of your Teacher. You have drawn within and you are keeping company with the Angelic Messengers. You have left the worldly mind, as it were, outside the real self, you have drawn a line of demarcation between the Spiritual self and the Material self. You are then balanced on both planes.

Whatever work you are called upon to do in the world, whether it be to run an office, a factory, or a home; or whether it be one of the more menial tasks of life; it is your duty to perform it to the best of your ability. Then, when you enter the silence, you carry with you to your Father the sense of peace that comes from work well done. In course of time He then gives you the "Well done" on the physical plane. The soul is filled with more peace and joy, for that message opens up a far higher and more beautiful understanding of the Inner Life. As the Chela progresses further along the path, his understanding becomes clearer; because, by contact with his Masters in his meditation, there has come the knowledge that all souls incarnate in matter are striving to reach God and at-one-ment with God, along the same road, but on different Rays and in different ways.

As you reach out, try to remember your past lives; picture your growth from mineral, through plant and animal, to man. Visualize the progress you have made, and if you work on these lines, scene after scene will flash into consciousness. You will see the mistakes you have made in the past and how to avoid them in the future. This interior clairvoyance is called "The Night of Tribulation," and it shows the soul remembering the past and its mistakes. It comes to everybody in the process of time, but it only comes when there is an entire separation of the everyday Conscious self from the Inner Spiritual self. You cannot blend spirit and matter. You can sometimes bring spirit through to matter, but it is not wise to do so in the early stages. Ascertain your Ray, and find everything that vibrates to you, such as mineral, colour, bird, animal, etc. You do this through your knowledge of the stars and numbers. Work it out for yourself; every time you ask another person to do it for you, you are lagging on the path. You are here to become self-individualized, self-sufficient and self-reliant. No one can become a Magian until he has developed the power of the will, and no one can develop the will if he depends upon another for everything. The more you develop the will, the greater your strength to overcome the lower personality. Again, in the development of the will, in time you will be able to command the inhabitants of the elemental kingdoms, and so to come into contact with those who live in the higher ethereal realms. From all I have said you will see how essential it is to separate the conscious every day from the Super-conscious, because by so doing you learn to function on two planes—spirit and matter. As you learn to control the will, more veils are removed, and you begin to see, to hear, and to hold converse with your Master.

QUESTIONS

Q. I-Em-Hotep, I understood you to say that we might consider ourselves your Chelas, and You our Guru. You now say that a Chela should bring his questions to his Guru. Do you mean us to do that in meditation?

A. No, my daughter, not until you have advanced to the state where you can hold converse with your Master in the spirit; therefore, you will be wise to bring all your questions to me, who am your Guru. When you have progressed further you will be able to hold converse with your Master in the spirit. Listening to the problems of Chelas will help you, when *you* become a Guru, to understand something of their type of mind, their state of development, and the Ray upon which each Chela is working.

Q. What is it that forms such a wonderful link between Guru and Chela?

A. Who, having gone through great dangers, trials and experiences with another for many incarnations, ever loses the memory of that friendship? Surely, time makes the tie stronger.

Q. Does the whole of the spirit incarnate?

A. That depends a great deal upon the type of spirit. The more advanced the spirit the less of it incarnates.

Q. If a soul in this day of life has very little leisure for meditation, would that mean that in a previous day of life it had practised meditation in an unlawful way?

A. Not necessarily, my daughter. Sometimes a soul has made great progress and loved another deeply. When the loved one re-incarnates, it often happens that the progressed soul also re-incarnates in order to be with the beloved. This

type of progressed soul might elect to abstain
from meditation because it had chosen to learn
the lesson of service.

Q. Would you have us to attack the problem of
meditation in a positive state of mind, or should
we endeavour to become receptive?

A. I dislike the receptive attitude, especially for
those in water signs, who become the prey of
lower astral forces that sweep them hither and
thither like a tide and make them a restless
stormy sea. It is far better for those of this
nature to begin to use Yoga practices and make
affirmations and visualisations. For an energetic fiery sign to strive to still the mind and
become receptive is good, but not water signs.
Again I would remind you that each person
must tread the path in a different way. The
fiery, energetic one must learn tranquility; the
patient water sign must learn activity; the air
sign that blows hither and thither must learn
balance; the earth sign must learn not to become fussy or hard, but soft and yielding.

Q. If a Horoscope show a lack of planets in Fire
or Earth signs, should the Native concentrate
upon the attributes of the Fire and earth signs
or should he endeavour to develop the qualities
of Air and Water?

A. My child, that would depend very much upon
how the planets are placed. It would also depend upon the Triangle of Ascent and the Triangle of Descent. If a Horoscope is at all un-

balanced, showing more planets in, shall we
say, Earth and Water signs, then, certainly you
should try to cultivate the attributes of Fire and
Air. For instance, if there was a preponder-
ance of Water and Earth, we might find that
the soul, instead of emanating peace, would be
full of fussy, grudging service. Therefore, it
would need some of the Fire of love, and some
of the cleansing of Air, to give warmth and
unity. Does that help you? Water signs have
the quality of being self-centred. People having
Water signs are constantly seeing their own
reflections. They are like Narcissus, inasmuch
as they often fall in love with their own reflections. Those who have a predominance of
Water signs would do well to cultivate the
quality of unselfishness, and endeavour to become more introspective.

Q. In a certain Horoscope which I have in my
mind, there are no planets in Fire or Earth signs,
but only in Air and Water, therefore, should
the lesson be to endeavour to acquire the qualities of Earth and Fire? In this particular Horoscope, the Air signs predominate with a Water
sign rising.

A. In the Horoscope I think you have in your
mind, there is a certain selfishness due to the
predominance of the Water sign personality.
There is the reflective quality which shows,
shall we say, a certain self-pity. Therefore,
the Native should develop a more universal love

element rather than one which is personal.
She should endeavour to draw all to her and be
interested in all. She should seek to unify all.
Instead of using the Air quality in the destructive sense, she should use it in the unifying
sense.

It is well sometimes to discuss what might
be our strength and our weakness, for on the
Path we are inclined to be unconscious hypo-
crites. We do not like our neighbours to know
our weaknesses, we only like them to know our
strength, but in asknowledging our weakness,
we are acting upon a saying of the Master
Jesus, " He who confesses his sins, the Father
is faithful and just to forgive his sins " ; and a
fault brought out to the light of day ceases to be
deeply imbedded in the nature. It is like the
butterfly that passes through the garden on a
Summer's day : it is there for a little time, and
then it is gone.

Q. When you spoke of the Triangles of Ascent
and Descent, did you mean the rulership of the
sign at the apex of the two Triangles, and not
the ones at the base?

A. That is so, my son.

Q. How do we find out to which Ray we belong?

A. One would have to see the Horoscope to decide the Ray to which you belong. It is the
Ray of the sun. If your Sun, shall we say, is
in Sagittarius, that is the Ray of the Spirit.
The Spirit has come from the Heaven-Worlds

of Jupiter; and in descending into matter the Moon may be in Libra with, perhaps, the sign Capricorn rising. In that case, you have come, shall I say, with all the Spiritual force, all the grandeur of the Jupiterian Ray, expressing itself on the Blue Ray of the Seraphim, whilst the Moon in Libra expresses the emotional unbalance of the sign. Therefore you have come to strengthen the Libran trait, to find balance on the emotional and the astral planes. You come with a Capricornian personality, that you may meet the Dweller on the Threshold, and experience all the trials and tests of that meeting; perhaps contacting " the Dweller " as Saturn the Tester, that you may return home to your Father-in-Heaven with the Saturnian force transmuted, the emotions steady, the experience on the astral wolds all garnered in and returned as peace, dignity and wisdom. Again, I repeat, you descend into matter through the Sun Ray; the Soul, which has to garner experience on the astral or the emotional planes, is expressed through the Moon Ray; through the Personality, which is the Ascendant, experience is garnered for the uplifting of the Soul, and returned with the fruits of the Soul and the experience garnered by the Personalty—back to the Father-in-Heaven.

Q. Would the Sun sign always be the same?

A. No, my daughter. When you have learned all the lessons of a sign, then the spirit descends through another sign of the Zodiac. It may be helpful to imagine ourselves to be in a Courtyard where there is a fountain so arranged that the water comes up through the top and spreads itself as it falls through twelve compartments of different coloured lights, into a pond below. He who is manipulating the water tap can turn it in the direction of the blue, green, yellow, or other colour, and the water as it passes through each colour, reflects its light in the pond below. The colour seen in the pond is not really the colour of the water; it is only made to appear so by the will of the manipulator. And so when the Sun comes in the sign of Virgo, shall we say, it is not really the only Ray. The spirit is beyond and above that sign, but it sends its Ray through the sign the better to help the soul and personality to garner its experience.

Q. For many months I have had dreams of a very vivid nature, and now I think I perceive their spiritual interpretation, but it seems presumptious to think that I remember instructions received in the sleep state?

A. Why should it seem presumptious? Look upon it as being something for which you should praise God, in as much that you are able to remember and bring into matter the experiences of the spiritual realms. As far as imagination is concerned, it is wise to realise that you are a spirit, functioning in a spiritual way, both consciously and un-consciously in different states, and at time able to bring through into your every-day mind the memory of events experienced in another state of consciousness. Speak of these thoughts and experiences, whether of the Earth or of the spirit, or those which come to you in your meditation, as states of consciousness. To every strata of mind are many states of consciousness.

Q. Is illness in the physical body a sign of spiritual failure?

A. Not necessarily in this life. If you come into incarnation and at a certain period you suffer from physical disability, you may have arranged to meet your karma at that particular time; it may be that you have arranged to work off family karma, or national karma. It is not always personal karma. Sometimes a member of a large family falls ill and tries hard to get well; in such a case, it may be that the condition of illness is to teach others forbearance, love and understanding. When those lessons have been learned, the soul is released from its karma because of its voluntary act in taking on that karma. Thus, the other members of the family receive a lesson and grow in understanding; whilst the suffering soul works out its karma.

Q. In what especial way do the initiatory methods of today differ from those used five thousand years ago?

A. In my day we accepted students for initiation
when they were quite young, sometimes in
their teens, and they remained in the Temple
or Monastery until they were quite old men. At
that period, all Temple Dwellers knew that the
time spent on Earth was a preparation for the
higher life, therefore, the pleasures of the body
were regarded as being of secondary importance. Our priests became doctors, elders,
teachers or mediums, and they all lived in the
enclosures of the Temple. Today you have an
exoteric religion and also an esoteric religion,
which you mix up and scatter around to all in
your world. In my time the esoteric teaching
was given only to those who were undergoing
special training. We had a school of education
in the outside world, and the teaching was
based upon spiritual lines, certain classes being
reserved for those who were preparing to enter
the Temple. No slaves were accepted in the
Temple as those who had re-incarnated in the
labouring classes were not considered to be
sufficiently advanced spiritually to understand
the teaching or pass the tests necessary for
priesthood; but craftsmen of certain grades
could become lay-brothers in the monasteries.
We kept the outer and the inner teaching very
separate. We lived in a continual state of
preparation for death. Whereas, today, you
only think of death as something to be avoided.
For us, it was the gateway leading to a Higher

Life.

Q. I-Em-Hotep, are you suggesting that the people of that time—five or six thousand years ago—were spiritually in advance of the people of today?

A. That is rather a difficult question, my friend. I would not suggest that the people of any one dynasty were necessarily in advance of those belonging to another. There were some souls in my day in Egypt who far surpassed any in your world today, but there were also some of a very low grade. Always, since humanity began to walk on two feet there have been souls in different states of evolution; also it must be remembered that in that remote period of time, not so very far removed from the Atlantean civilization, the Sons of God were still incarnating for the teaching of humanity.

Q. From the excavations that we have been able to make and examine it would seem that you knew infinitely more about the inner science than we do today?

A. Although you are making progress, I must say that we were in advance of the scientists of your day in as much as we were able to harness the Cosmic Rays, a thing that you are not able to do.

Q. How came such a discovery to be lost, I-Em-Hotep?

A. My daughter, the Gods, watching humanity and human desires and frailties, sometimes deem it wise to make it lose its memory of things. If it were for the good of evolution, or of the world at the moment, that the method of harnessing the Cosmic Rays should be redis-covered, then such method would quickly be given to a receptive mind, but your world today is so filled with hatred of man, one for another, that any such rediscovery would be used as a force for destruction rather than as a force for healing. You are going through a night of time, you must understand; but when the dawn arrives, many things shall be rediscovered.

PRAYER

Oh Thou who art the giver of light! Pour forth Thy heavenly food and fire to cleanse and nourish the hearts and minds and souls of these Thy children. Fill themwith Thy holy spirit; make them receptive to the inflow of Thy wisdom. Let Thy peace and Thy love surround them in all their ways. Fill them with the spirit of earnestness, of peace and joy.

Oh most holy Mother, gather them in as a mother gathers into her arms her tired children, and give them sweet refreshment and repose. Strengthen their spirits, and give them courage to tread the more interior way. Amen.

DAILY LIFE ON THE PATH

TO-NIGHT our subject is "Daily life on the Path," and at the outset please understand that there are no hard and fast rules laid down. You must take my words and apply them to your own especial needs, because each one is in a different environment, has a different character, and different ideals. Therefore, whilst we speak of the Path, it would be better perhaps to speak of the goal, because the goal is the same for all, but there are twelve paths that lead to it, and so aspirants for Initiation stand on the twelve-fold path and have twelve different ideals of the Godhead. In the Western world, naturally, your ideal is Jesus of Nazareth. He has for some hundreds of years been portrayed to you as "Man made perfect," therefore, when I speak to you of exercises and of coming into at-one-ment with God, you must choose your own personification of God, because when you begin to live the life of an Initiate on the Path, no matter in what environment you find yourself, whether it be in cottage or palace, always you have to remember that success on the Way of Attainment is not measured by what the lips are saying but by what the heart is thinking.

And so, my friends, the first essential thing towards coming into at-one-ment, is to find out your own particular ideal of God. To some it may be Buddha, to other Jesus, Krishna, the Virgin, Confucius, Kwanyin, Mohammed, Muriel or Horus. With all these different aspects you should choose the type that appeals the most to you. Since you are of the Western world, no doubt you will prefer to take the type of perfection that you are taught is in Jesus of Nazareth.

Having chosen your ideal of God, it is necessary to learn something of right meditation, so, I will now outline the technique of a meditation you may like to try.

First of all settle the question of time. If you are a worker you may prefer to choose the evening, but, for those who do not earn their daily bread the early morning will do. All unkind thoughts and all criticism must be eliminated from your mind. Make the whole of your nature vibrant with love; love for all beings irrespective of what they may be; love for all creatures no matter to what kingdom they may belong; thus you will fill the mind with nothing but love. Follow this by taking a bath to cleanse the body, so that we start our meditation with thoughts of love, cleansing with water, which is symbolical of spirit. Then, if possible, put on a clean white garment of any material to symbolize the loosening or riddance of old habits and conditions and the donning of the robe of righteousness.

In the East, the aspirant who meditates usually sits on a mat, because he can take it with him if he goes on a journey. The mat is a holy place, so those of you who have not a room or sanctuary can obtain a rug or mat, which should be four-square, because on it you are going to build your holy temple. When your meditation is over, you can fold or roll your mat and put it carefully away. You will suppose you now have your mat ready and in the centre you take the posture of the Yogi with the spine erect and the legs folded. So seated on your mat you begin to take for your meditation some picture of one of the holders of the Christ power. We have decided it shall be Jesus of Nazareth—I, myself, cannot think of a more wonderful and beautiful ideal of the Master Jesus than that which was painted by Hoffmann. You now concentrate your thought upon the Master Jesus, and as you begin to memorize every line of the face, to note the look in his eyes, and the way the hands are held, you should begin to feel that you are becoming merged into the personality of Jesus. His words, actions and thoughts, beat in upon your mind the more you identify yourself with him. When you have made further progress you will find yourself withdrawing from the physical body, and in place of yourself, you should see it clothed with the thought substance which you have emanated during the picturization of your Master. At a later stage, when you withdraw more completely from your physical body, you will perceive that you have clothed your physical vehicle in an emanation of Godhead, at the same time obtaining an exterior form of consciousness. Herein lies the danger, because having withdrawn a little from the

E.

physical body, you are becoming a fourth-dimensional being; you are beginning to see on the plane of the fourth dimension, and you must remember that this plane is governed by the lower Neptunian forces. Therefore, you are functioning on the plane of illusion and you will frequently find that in the early testing days in your new world you will be accosted by beings who seem to be Angels of Light, because these beings approach you, trailing, as it were, robes of glory, hailing you with seductive voices, whispering in your ears that you have accomplished something at last, in that you are functioning on another plane of consciousness. You must never listen to any one, no matter how bright or how wonderful in appearance, if the accosting entity cannot answer you in a like way as you invoke the Name of God. For your Christian ways, you make the sign of the cross; for the Eastern ways, the sign of the pentagram; because those who are not truly spirits of greatness must disintegrate or reveal their true selves before the sign of the cross or the sign of the pentagram. I want you to remember this particularly, because to every aspirant on the Path there comes a test in the form of a great temptation. Your pride tells you how wonderful you are to be able to leave your body and meet these spirits of brightness who have nothing but fair words for you, but watch with suspicion, and challenge every one you meet out of the body; bid them stand, in the three-fold name of God, and answer you with the sign of the Cross.

If they cannot do this, they must answer you with the pentagram, and if they fail to do so, then you must let them go and return to your body as quickly as possible, and so finish your meditation for that day.

In meditation, do not take an abstract thing and let your mind become unmanageable; do not empty the mind or let it become negative, because when you first begin to practise meditation, if you sit, quietly waiting for thoughts to come into your mind, you are being filled with the reflections of the astral plane; nothing builds up strongly or concretely, therefore your thought force is wasted. That is why I have tried to show you a method by which you identify yourself with an aspect of God-head. Do not think, when I advise you to visualize the Master Jesus and to clothe yourself in His personality, thus striving to image yourself with Him, that I am asking you to do something which is sacrilege, because the main idea in your mind is to attain at-one-ment with God. You cannot do this unless you form some conception of God, but if, time after time, you identify yourself with one of His Messengers, you gradually climb the ladder that brings you nearer, and in the end your spirit is merged with Him-Her.

The Master Jesus taught His disciples a meditation known as "The washing of the feet." You have already received this meditation,* which is

* See Appendix.—Ed.

also known as the meditation of I.A.O. Now
I.A.O. was the mystical name given by Jesus to
His Father in Heaven. If we look into its inner
meaning we shall see that " I " represents Isis, the
Mother aspect, " A " symbolizes Apophis the
Destroyer or the Guardian of the underworld, and
" O " stands for Osiris. With this knowledge we
concentrate on the three-fold aspect of God, regarding Himas Father-Mother-Son, light-darkness
and love, remembering that the Lord of the Underworld watches, weighs and tests the soul before it
can send the light.

As you meditate day after day and focus your
thoughts upon your beloved Master Jesus, you
gradually grow more like Him in your nature. This
statement may give rise to the question : " How are
we to know that this result has been attained?"
The answer is that your meditation has brought
about a certain union with the Master, with whom
you have chosen to come into at-one-ment. You
commence to emanate a power that is felt by others.
You are more serene, the petty trials and temptations of life no longer distress or annoy you, you
are balanced on all planes of consciousness. You
are able to curb and transmute your emotions ; they
no longer toss you about as on a wild and restless
sea, but rather are you caught up in the supreme
love, and are resting in a calm and peaceful bay.
You will find that the nearer you are to the goal
of attainment the less likely you are to air a
little knowledge you have; the less likely are

you to try to make yourself unlike your neigh bours, because the true Initiate and the true Adept seek to mingle with all whom they contact. They do not flaunt the symbols of their order; they do not wear mysterious-looking jewels, they are serene and strong in the strength of the Almighty; and only through the balance and serenity of mind, the peace and love that emanate from them, can you be sure that you have met the one who is on the Path, even as you.

Returning to the subject of our meditation, I would say that during your out-of-the-body state, you may possibly meet and recognise other aspirants on the Path. In this way you learn to see each other as you really are; you learn to love each other because you are all aspects of Godhead; you forget to crticise the faults of the personality, you forget to be inharmonious, you forget petty jealousies and annoyances; you begin to live as the Master you seek at-one-ment with, and day by day you find yourselves becoming more emptied of the self and more filled with God. I do hope this does not sound too improbable to you. Your Master Jesus, I have taught you, is still in a body, and still seeks to do the will of His Father, and as you seek to identify yourself with the the image of Him that has been created, cannot you realize how His love will reach out to you; how He will become your guardian and your helper during all your days on earth? Can you not feel the joy and love coming from Him to you when He realizes that you are seeking to tread the very path He trod, and that you are seeking to bring into manifestation the things He tried to bring into manifestation? Surely as the knowledge of this method of identifying oneself with one's Master spreads and grows, then all the great Masters of the past must reach out to you, and your world will become again what God our Father-Mother intended—a place of peace and joy, where war shall cease and harmony and love pervade everything. There will be no need for your hearts to be torn because of cruelty to the animal kingdom, because when man has reached perfection, this planet will have evolved to a point where it will not be necessary for the animal creation to continue. Therefore, take heart, and commence to identify yourself with your aspect of God, personified in your Master.

QUESTIONS

Q. I-Em-Hotep, how long should we take over this meditation?

A. Do not trouble about time, because we are now entering a state of consciousness where time does not exist. See that you are alone and undisturbed. Let your soul govern the time that you are out of the body. If you think about time your mind is divided; you cannot wholly lose consciousness of a plane or of yourself. If you commence, as I have said, it will take you at least, I suppose, half an hour.

Before completing your preliminary preparations, see that you have a small light; do not sit in darkness. Then, compose the self and try to image the face of your Master, and His type of personality. Let your thoughts be filled entirely with your Master. You may not lose consciousness the first time you sit, but the minute your thoughts begin to wander away from your Master, then stop. Do not allow the mind to enter into any other grove of thought. You see, I want you to be very careful, because once you strive to attain wisdom, and try to become a force for good in the world, you naturally become more and more sensitive, and you may become the prey of very subtle opposing thought forces of the type that are used by the grey brothers. Immediately your mind begins to wander away from your Master to other things, stop your meditation for that sitting. Those who have been accustomed to meditation, may leave their body the first time they sit. Those who have not practised this form of meditation may have to exercise perseverance.

You must remember that these are preliminary classes, and in treading the three-fold path you start by treading the path of mysticism. You are taking the Master Jesus, and in your meditation you must try not to let your thoughts wander from His sayings and His personality. If we cannot develop psychically, then we try to develop on the mystic path ; when the mystic path fails, we try to develop on the occult path, knowing that one is for us.

Q. May we meditate on a Master other than the Master Jesus?

A. Those of you who come into contact with another Master may certainly medidate upon that Master, in the same way, and clothe your self with His personality. The Unknowable Creator of us all has sent from time to time, many messengers or emanations of Himself. To me it matters little which Ray of Him-Her I worship, since I can worship the whole and worship Him-Her also; but for you I chose the Master Jesus, because in your Western religion you are accustomed to regard Him as your especial emanation of Godhead.

Q. Suppose a Chela finds the Yogi posture difficult or is frightened that he may topple over?

A. My son, I would suggest the posture usually adopted by the Master with whom you are trying to come into at-one-ment. The Master Jesus usually sat, and rested His arm thus— finger to cheek, making the sacred sign of protection. That is an easy posture. With regard to the second portion of your question, let me explain, that no aspirant on the path is left ungarded, during meditation. Whilst you are under my instruction, everyone of you has a watcher, a guardian; and such a one will see that no harm comes to the aspirant. Each Teacher has his own method; I can only answer for mine.

Q. I-Em-Hotep. What are the stages on the path leading to Mastership?

A. An aspirant or seeker is one who has tried many paths, none of which satisfy. These paths may include the intellectual examination of many philosophies, religion and occult teachings. He realizes that there are other plane of consciousness or he may have psychic experiences; again he may have seen materializations in the séance room and, finding that these things did not satisfy, he seeks that which lies beyond spiritualism, and is called its Inner or Higher Teaching. When he has been an aspirant for some time he usually attaches himself to some teacher, and after he has assimilated the teaching he becomes a neophyte, and in time is drawn to a higher grade, through a Ceremony, Baptism or Ritual, and is received into the Ray of his Teacher, thus becoming an Initiate of that Ray. He then goes through the higher teaching and cleansing of the Ray, gradually working up to the stage higher, viz. the grade of "Adeptus Minor," and so on. You see how wonderful God is. He gives you freedom to choose your Ray, and the Teacher associated with that Ray, and all that is expected from you is obedience whilst you are on that Ray. If through pride or other faults you fail and turn against your teacher, then the powers of darkness have gained a foothold into an erstwhile pure community. The Master Jesus overcame His temptations largely by the strength He obtained through meditation. He sought to identify Himself with God, with Moses, Elijah, and the prophets. It was said that by His loyalty and love, He had drawn two shining ones to Him.

Q. If you have attained to a grade of Initiation, does that mean that you have not to go through it again?

A. No, my daughter; having attained to a certain grade of Initiation, you may have reached adeptship on one Ray, and that will be quickly recognised by your Teacher. Then you will be given instruction on another Ray, and perhaps see things from a different angle.

Q. I have been accustomed to look upon Moses and Elijah as lesser representations of the Deity than Jesus of Nazareth?

A. That is only because of the time, my son. Moses in His day was quite as great as the Master Jesus. He led those who were in bondage to freedom, and Jesus sought to do the same.

In your movement of Spiritualism to-day, you have Teachers such as Power, Redcloud, White Hawk, White Eagle, White Feather, Silver Fox, and many others; all striving to do the same work. Some of this teaching has been recorded and will be preserved for long periods of time, also, there will be precepts handed down in families. In five hundred years from now, who is to say which of these Teachers was the greatest Master. I do not like being personal, but in my own day and time I founded my Temple of Healing and began to tread the mystic way. I came into at-one-ment with the Godhead, and in the fullness of time I was gathered to Him. From three to five hundred years after I had entered the world of spirit, the Egyptians made a God of me. Can you not realise how much myth and speculation and fancy was mingled with the act that made me a God?

Q. Why is it that we do not receive the truth when the soul of the world is crying out for it?

A. The soul of the world cries out for truth, but when truth is sent, humanity rejects it. Humanity requires truth to be dressed in its own clothing; therefore truth may be likened to a diamond with many facets. Your idea of truth, my daughter, would be quite different from that of another person. Not until there is more harmony and more unity can truth be unveiled.

Q. Today our patriotism seems to get narrower and more limited. I wonder if in ancient days the expression of patriotism could be traced to those who occupied the same astrological sign?

A. It has been narrowed down to synchronize with racial limitation. In the early days of Atlantis, there were twelve states, each governed by a king, and the king was guided by the Divine Hierophant or Christed One, the Outer manifestation of the Great Architect of the Universe. Each king sought to unify and strengthen the people in his special state that all the other states might benefit, the main object being to carry out the wishes of the Divine Hierophant. In your world today, we find many of your states at war, their rulers fighting largely for power or territory. The source of all war is usually to be found in some form of greed. You may ask what causes this, and what has separated you in the beginning? It is your different aspect of religion. When there is a greater degree of brotherhood in your world, you will build a universal religion.

PRAYER

Oh, Thou Divine Essence of Love, flow into the hearts of these Thy children. Illuminate them that they may touch Thee on the higher planes of consciousness. Reveal Thyself to them. Let Thy peace calm their minds. Let them feel the sweet influence of the Mother aspect of Thee helping them, and teach them to revere all that Thou hast given to them of joy, or sorrow, of pain and gladness. Help them to realize that Thou hast considered them worthy of regeneration. Give them courage and strength to go forward in the new future, filled with the thought Thou art with them

and they with Thee. Help them to rely on Thy
guidance, help them to feel one with Thee. Bless
each one and give unto them Thy food that they
may feed the hungry, give to them the waters of
Thy spirit that they may give to those who are
athirst. Touch their eyes and their ears. Help
them to be harbingers of Light. Bring all things to
their remembrance that they fear not again, Oh
Thou who has called us together, incarnate and
discarnate, help Thy children to grow strong that
they may do the work Thou hast given them to do.
Let them not grow weary. Let them faint not. Let
them not be disheartened and let not Set have
power to darken their minds. Let health and
strength and power and love and peace and wisdom be their portion. I, thy servant, ask this for
these Thy children. So be it.

THE TRAINING OF THE MIND

TO-NIGHT, my subject is "The Training of the Mind." As you know, the mind is the receiver of all material thoughts and impressions; it is also the channel for the expression of all spiritual thought and impressions, therefore, it may be asked, "where is the dividing line?" And so to convey to you a clearer picture we will divide the mind into four imaginary planes and call them the Super-conscious mind, the Psychic mind, the Sub-conscious or Astral mind, and the Conscious or Physical mind. The Super-conscious mind pertains to the Etheric and belongs to the higher plane of the upper mental, the Psychic mind to the lower plane of the upper mental, the Sub-conscious mind to the higher plane of the lower mental, and the Conscious mind to the physical or lower plane of the lower mental, the conscious waking mind is concerned with all that belongs to the physical plane and it is in the conscious mind that you learn to express your thoughts in the language of the country in which you may reside. It is through the medium of the sub-conscious that you are able to transmit to the conscious mind all that partakes of the psychic and the super-conscious minds. The sub-conscious is the bridge dividing the conscious mind from both the psychic and the super-con-

scious minds and it is in the sub-conscious mind
that you have reflections of all planes above and
all planes below.

A good example of the action of the sub-conscious mind is to be found in the person who is
under hypnosis, for, in such a case the sub-conscious mind is reflecting from the psychic and the
spiritual minds all the knowledge that has been
garnered in the past days of life. The conscious
mind being at rest or asleep, cannot interfere.

Although it may be a little at variance with that
of other teachers, you will now be better able to
understand my statement that the resting mind
pertains to the physical or conscious mind because
it is the mind man uses when he says, '' I want
things that I can see, that I can tabulate ''; whilst
the intuitions and instincts come from the Super-
conscious, and are transmuted through the Psychic mind down into the Sub-conscious, where
they react as an impulse or shall I say an
instinct—and unless the conscious mind inter-
feres with the faculties of the sub-conscious, all
things work out well. Should, however, the
conscious mind interfere, then you get a mixture
and distortion coming through the sub-conscious
bridge.

As we proceed I shall continue to use the
terms, sub-conscious, psychic, and super-conscious minds. Now you who are here, have
touched the sub-conscious through a desire to
develop in a psychic way; and some of you find

that you sit for development for a long time without result, and the reasoning mind or the conscious mind begins to say, " is there any truth in the existence of these super-physical realms, is it true that there are guides who control, can we really come into touch with a Master, or is it a figment of the imagination?"   Thus the conscious reasoning mind begins to crowd the sub-conscious mind until it becomes utterly false and unable to reflect the teaching that comes through from the super-physical realms, with the result that you may have a sense of breaking down, a feeling of physical depression, and your faith is reduced to zero.   You should now realize through the working of the conscious, reasoning mind, that the mind has four compartments or divisions; that each division is governed by an Angel Watcher or a guide and that you can train your conscious mind to receive messages from each of these divisions or planes of mind through your Masters or guides; then you are clearing away the false and becoming at once receptive to the messages from these higher planes of mind, but no one can open the door except yourself.

The time for unconscious mediumship is passing.   You are living in an age that is governed by air signs, therefore it is the mediumship of the mental plane that will in future be used by the Lords who govern the destiny of this planet. Thus, it behoves all who are interested in the service of humanity, to train the mind to become receptive to the higher mental plane so that they can receive teaching; but, until they can receive such teaching from their own Masters or guides and be sure it is not their imagination, they must study on the physical plane. Study on the physical plane will help immensely. For instance, some of you who are studying in the ritual classes have sometimes remarked to your fellow students, "I can't see the use of it, it seems a lot of rubbish to me." Thus speaks the conscious mind that is ignorant of the super-physical conditions. You may be only engaged in drawing a pentagram, in very laboriously writing Hebrew characters, or it may be counting the inches that go to the making of a circle or square, but behind all that, by the concentration along that one particular line, you are "developing" in the super-conscious and psychic minds. You are training the psychic and super-conscious minds to come, as it were, into the vibration of earth; and as you go on concentrating on apparently useless symbols, so are you setting up that separative quality in the mind which is necessary to hold the conscious, reasoning mind in abeyance while you function on a mental, psychic and super-physical plane. It is certainly through the procedure of concentration that upon receiving your first illumination, and seeing the sigils and the symbols reflected in the etheric light, you begin to realize that a pentagram means more than a five-pointed star; it means that there is some one on the mental plane flashing messages to you.

F

You have learned the symbolism of colour, therefore you are able to guage, by the colour represented, the type of entity that wishes to commune
with you. You know whether it is an elemental,
a disembodied spirit or a Governor of a Ray; you
know whether it is one of the Earls or one of the
Lords of a planet, and so, having learnt to still the
conscious mind and be receptive in the psychic and
super-conscious minds, you are ready for the inflow
of wisdom from the one who has sought you out
in order to teach you; but, remember, no knowledge comes to you unless you train the mind to
be receptive.

You are now passing out of the psychic or
Neptunian Age, and during the last fifty years of
that age people were strongly under the Neptunian
influence, thus psychism was able to make headway; but in the next fifty years, the Air Age will
bring about a development of mental mediumship.
Psychic mediumship has played its part. It has
brought man to a higher stage of consciousness; it
has lifted him out of the materialism of the Neptunian Age into the realism of the higher Rays of
Neptune, and now, the blending of these higher
Rays of Neptune with the Air of Aquarius under
the rulership of Uranus, will bring to the minds of
men a great influx of spiritual knowledge. There
shall be that pouring out of spirit upon all mankind that has been foretold, but first, you have to
work in the house of the body, clearing out the
rooms that will be required so that they will be

ready for your inspirers.

To obtain the best results either in business or with work that is done with the hands, the mind must be working properly. The time, however, has now come when you should realize that work done through the instrumentality of the brain, can be influenced by the Higher Mind, and this influence can be brought through the Psychic and Subconscious minds into the conscious mind. It is hoped that in the future, inspiration may pour into man's conscious mind, making the Aquarian Age, one of great inventions, an Age when mankind will be inspired in a high degree. Man will no longer be held back by the idea that unless every " i " is dotted and every " t "crossed, it cannot be true. He will learn spiritual values and be able to bring into the consciousness teaching from the Cosmic Mind. In time he will be able to touch the realms in which those Beings are able to function who are the Lords that govern humanity, who are the Masters; and come into conscious hearing, sight and touch. All this without the use of the ectoplasm that is necessary to-day in your materialising séances. As soon as you raise your consciousness to the fourth dimensinal state, the atoms of which your body is composed—its very cell formation—will begin to change. The whole of the body will take on a higher rate of vibration and you will become aware of other states of consciousness. You will be able to contact your Master or your Teacher whilst sitting in your sanctuary or your armchair in a way that is comparable to the manner in which to-day you can see life portrayed upon the screen when you go to a cinema.   In like fashion your Master can portray for you in the etheric light the laws that govern evolution, the lessons that pertain to the elemental kingdoms and the lessons that pertain to the spiritual kingdoms. In this etheric light, as soon as you have raised your consciousness to where you can perceive those things, you become mentally clairvoyant.   Mental clairvoyance is the state of development aimed at by all occultists because the mediumship is then of a higher character, the instrument or medium being able to contact the spiritual realms whilst still in a conscious state.

Trance mediumship, whilst it is of value to-day, will be in abeyance in the future, and the ear of man will be able to hear when man has raised his vibrations to where the voice of the Master can be heard, and there will be a relaying of my voice to you instead of my coming to you through my instrument.   To-day my instrument, when in full consciousness, is capable of repeating to you my words to her, but she informs me that it is a method of transmission not yet fully understood, for you have not quite yet grasped the fact that one is able to transmit knowledge from the spiritual realms just as one would transmit a message through a telephone or by means of radio communication.

Every one of you in this room is a potential re- ceiver, and that, apart from psychic development,

the psychic mind can become tuned in to the super-
physical realms or super-conscious mind and you
can relay through the sub-conscious to the conscious mind the pictures and words received. Once
you have reached this state of mental development,
nothing is hidden from you, but before control of
this mental mediumship is given to you, you have
to prove yourself worthy to receive, because as you
attune your mind and purify your bodies so are
you entrusted with the laws by which the universe
is governed and your mind is used for the repro-
duction of things that will aid humanity towards
perfection, but these laws will never be entrusted
to you if you are out for self-aggrandisement or if
you seek to impress others. If, however, you are
obedient and striving to work in harmony with the
Masters and the Gods, then you are at once used
by them for the furtherance of evolution on your
planet. The Gods have been betrayed many times
by evolving units of humanity who have never
developed the Divine Spark, but who wanted to
cut very fine figures in the only world they knew.
Those who seek to make themselves great in the
eyes of man you may be very sure have never
known the company of the Angel world. The
man who has descended from the Angel kingdoms
and has developed the Divine Spark within him
through many ages of evolution is aware of the joy
and wonders to be found upon other planets, for
it is a part of his training. He is fully aware that
this little dark plane of yours is but a testing

ground, a school of experience, and he seeks not to shine as a peacock strutting before others, but always to lift and to emulate all with whom he comes in contact. Throughout the history of the world, you will find that the Christed Ones have given up the things of the world and sought the things of the spirit. By their simple lives they have sought to teach their followers that it is not the goods of the world that brings peace or glorification, but the things of the spirit.

Those who are truly helping humanity work quietly, and working quietly, unobtrusively and unselfishly will, in course of time, receive the Christ Power, a Power which draws all men to them, because every Christed One is like a magnet so filled with the Spirit of God that it attracts all those who have the Divine Spark awake. When the command is given to a Christed One to go out and teach the masses, then to that One is given the Power to work miracles, in order that those who witness the miracles may be impressed when they see the Power of God manifesting through a personality. Demonstrations of this nature, however, are very rare.

I suggest that you endeavour to train your mind in a quiet and reverent way in order that you may come into touch with the higher forces, then will such peace, such beauty, and such wisdom be yours that you will not find it necessary to seek those you would aid, for you are gently led to where you can help the hungry and thirsty souls, and you are filled with such power and strength that you are able to send your mind afar for the helping and healing of others.

The greatest gift our Divine Father-Mother has given to His-Her children is the gift of mind; but for many generations, minds have been sleeping and they are only just awakening and emerging from that age-long sleep. Your medical men are beginning to understand psychology. Your spirit friends are beginning to understand that they can influence the mind plane; and unconsciously you are helping in that development because as you seek after wisdom, so do you open up on the planes of mind and slowly the truth percolates through.

Many of you here are beginning to say " I came into Spiritualism, I was interested for a while and then I wanted to learn something more," and so your guide on the psychic plane influenced you sub - consciously; finally your desire worked through to the conscious mind and you came seeking. You then began to vibrate on to the sub-conscious or astral mind. You are now vibrating on the psychic mind and beginning to vibrate on the super-conscious mind, and so, step by step, unconsciously, you are evolving on the planes of mind.

I do not know if I can teach you any more at the present stage about the planes of mind, but I do want you to realise that in order to fit yourselves for the inflow of knowledge from the Masters, Guides, and Planetary Regents, you have to work.

Therefore, again we come back to those so-called useless sciences : Astrology, Numbers, Sound and Colour. You must learn the language of these planes of mind if you would commune with the inhabitants thereon, so consider nothing wasted that you learn of number, sound, colour or planet. Strive to learn all you can and when you have learned all that your books can teach you, and you understand the symbols and the colouring, then you can begin to sit and ask for further instruction. If you strive earnestly, nothing is withheld so long as you are honest, pure and true in your desires, but seek none of these things if you desire power to forward your interest in the world, because you are still but a child playing with fire and the very forces that you invoke, if they are invoked for selfish purposes, shall in the end become your destroyers.

QUESTIONS

Q. I-Em-Hotep, would you say that the mind consists of four planes only?

A. No, my friend. Beyond the super-conscious mind is the Divine mind that resides in the heart of God. In your heart centre you are perfect for here is situated the Divine Spark of mind which is linked with the Divine Mind of God.

Q. I once saw your instrument take the communion service and noticed that she was swaying. Would that be caused by any power of mind?

A. When the communion is given by any of my

priests, I overshadow them to such an extent that they experience much discomfort. May I explain that it is my aura mingling with theirs that causes a feeling resembling slight dizziness.

Q. Can a Master use ordinary language when he speaks to a pupil on the plane of mind?

A. Symbols are always used on the mental plane; these symbols are taken up by the sub-conscious mind and transmuted into a language that the conscious mind can understand.

Q. I-Em-Hotep, will you tell me where the faculty of divination is generated?

A. The super-conscious mind having knowledge, transmits it to the psychic plane, where it is transmuted into symbolism perhaps of an astrological nature or even a reading of the Tarot cards, but it is the psychic mind that transmits the evidence or message through to the sub-conscious mind.

Q. It would appear that we cannot do away with the psychic faculty?

A. That is so. To do away with the psychic faculty is to do away with a road of approach. It has been a mistake of many occultists in the past to decry mediumship; it shows a lack of balance and it shows they are not fully developed occultists. The fully developed occultist knows that when he has learned to function on the super-conscious, psychic, sub-conscious and conscious planes, that there are still other realms to which he may aspire. He realizes that every plane of consciousness is but a resting place. Nothing must be left out for his perfect manifestation, but no more reliance must be placed upon one plane than another.

Q. In using another mind, is it valuable to an operator such as yourself if in that mind you find certain knowledge? Would it help you to express yourself better?

A. Of a surety, my son. As you know I have only been speaking through this instrument for about two years. I was fortunate in having helpers who prepared the mind so that it became receptive to the desire of the Gods. The instrument was so advanced that she sought to develop the brain and the body in order to become a better receiver. As we trained the instrument to become a receiver on the mental plane, we inspired her with a desire to do less and less on the psychic plane, and therefore, as she entered into co-operation with us, a certain amount of psychic work was necessary to interest people in the mental side; for this we had a loyal co-operator in that entity whom you know as White Hawk. He prepared the mind on one plane and we prepared it on the other, and for many years he gave our teaching until he had so rarified and impregnated the atoms that they became quickened to our rate of vibration and we were able to take control. Since we have taken control we have been able to teach the instrument while in the conscious state; therefore her mind is now receptive to any thought of ours, and understanding all symbolism is able to receive our messages. I might state here that some of you think our instrument is in many ways better equipped than you are. She is only better equipped in the sense that she possessed the quality of obedience, and there was never to our knowledge any spiritual pride for the furthering of her own ends. She was obedient to our commands and gradually she passed those tests and trials necessary for the development of mediumship for teaching in a conscious way. The reason she is subduing her personality now is because you, at your present state of evolution prefer at the moment to receive your teaching from a spirit control, but as we have explained, our instrument can hear our words when fully conscious, even as you will ultimately, when you become more advanced. I do not know if this explanation is disturbing or whether it illuminates.

Q. I-Em-Hotep, would you say that the reasoning faculty is an enemy to knowledge?

A. My daughter, the reasoning mind, or the analytcal faculty, is a great help, but not in cases when it gives rise to doubt.

Q. I have in mind a particular person who reasons everything out and will not accept teaching about reincarnation or things like that because he cannot see any reason for it?

A. My daughter, there are old souls and young souls; there are souls who have incarnated on another planet, but who are visiting the Earth for the first time. Having no memory of Earth, reincarnation strikes no chord of remembrance. I know there are some people who would reason that all knowledge lies in the sub-conscious mind. To say that knowledge can lie in one part of the brain and not in another is a thing that I cannot understand. The person you have mentioned may not be ready to receive spiritual truth. Supposing, for instance, you hear a clear voice giving you a command and you say " Well, this is perhaps imagination, why should I hear the Masters' voice. It may not be a voice at all." This attitude does not encourage the one who is seeking to help you. In our world we are not easily discouraged; we are often drawn near to a soul because of some spiritual affinity. We may have known them in the past or in the past have studied together. If they close their ears to our voice and say that we are all imagination, then we are sad because we know that we cannot touch them until their mind has awakened to the memory of the past or until the mind has become softened by grief.

Q. I-Em-Hotep, do the messages that are transmitted from the higher mind to the conscious mind come to us through the instrumentality of the guides or do they come through the mental plane?

A. It just depends, my son. If you are sitting for a psychic manifestation the guides of the psychic plane transmit the message; if you are sitting for a mental or a spiritual illumination, then the Master on the spiritual plane is able to reach you himself. Everybody arrives at a certain state of development through the efforts they have made, but later on they must have guidance.

Q. Is that guidance conscious?

A. It should be, you cannot make unconscious progress. There has been too much talk about Initiations on the inner planes, a favourite topic with the Neptunian person. Who can take an Initiation on the inner planes and be totally unaware of it? I have met people who claim to have partaken of these Initiations, but I have not seen the mark of the Initiate upon their brow, or found them wise, kind or charitable. They are usually very self-satisfied and smug when they hint of their Initiations on the inner planes. All Initiations must have an outer manifestation. When there is no outer manifestation and no improvement in the general character, then you may take it for certain that these claimants are being misled by some mischievous or elemental guide. I know some of you will not like it but since I come through to speak the truth I must present it as I perceive it.

Q. Will you give us an exercise that will stimulate the growth of the psychic mind?

A. Buy an Ephemeris for the current year, and from it find out the time of the New Moon. At the time of the New Moon commence your exercise by taking an upright position in a chair with the spine vertical and held erect and the head in line, elbows resting on the arms of the chair. After a time you will find that the head will be inclined to fall a little, so place a light book on your head to keep it erect, because all fluids must have an easy flow in the spine. Now you proceed to take the usual three nasal breaths in a rhythm of nine, but, because the left side of the body is ruled by the Moon, you inhale through the left nostril in three breaths; you hold for three, you exhale for three; you inhale again through the left nostril three hold three and exhale three, and again inhale three, hold three and exhale three. That is your nine breaths. You then imagine the Moon reflected in a pool of still water. During the whole four quarters of the Moon, you sit for a little while every day—a few moments will do. You do the nine breaths. You imagine the pool of water and build the first narrow semi-circular portion of the Moon, each day watching it grow larger in the pool until the Moon is full. During your meditation, on certain days you may see the forms of people, birds, or animals coming into the picture; if so, make a note of it. In time you will see more clearly and perhaps see something fresh every day. You can practise this exercise any time when the mind is tranquil. It is best to commence when the Moon is new, and as the Moon grows the psychic mind will reflect its real size into the pool. This is your first exercise in concentration on the psychic mind, but stop sitting if the mind begins to wander from the picture.

Q. I-Em-Hotep, supposing your horoscope shows a certain danger in touching psychic matters?

A. If your horoscope shows danger, you should on no account try to develop any psychic powers without some one to help you. If you place yourself under a qualified teacher, you are protected by the teacher's aura. To-night we are not dealing with psychic development, but are learning how to function in the psychic mind.

PRAYER

Oh Infinite Source of Wisdom. Thou who art our Mother, and did first teach us, Thy children, the wonders and the marvels of the Creative mind of our Father; speak to us, Thine unstable children and fill us with the wisdom of the higher realms. Cleanse our minds and so bring about a higher vibration in our bodies, until we are pure enough to hold converse with Thy ministering angels. Relieve these Thy children from all material cares, that they may draw near to Thee in spirit. Help them to be as Thou art, full of divine wisdom and love. Help them to share their love with the whole universe. Help them to give up all that is mean, all that is petty and small, all that is unworthy in their natures, that they may be the partakers of Thy light and love.

Oh Thou who hast loved us since the ages began, gather us in, Thy children incarnate and discarnate, for we seek to emulate Thee, Oh Most Divine, Oh Most Glorious. We seek to do Thy work on the earth plane, so strengthen us Thy discarnate ones that we may bring through a little of Thy divineness to these Thy children incarnate. Let the bridge that divides the two worlds no longer exist, that we may see each other as we truly are, and present each face to face with the other.

Send down Thy heavenly food and fire to nourish and cleanse and out of Thine abundance supply all things needful for spiritual and material growth. Gather us in, Oh Thou Divine Spirit, that we may feel the strength of the Father and the love of the Mother and the wisdom of the Son, that we may feel ourselves again as one family in Thine eternity. Bless each one and leave with them Thy peace. Amen.

THE TRAINING OF THE BODY

I HAVE already spoken about the training of the mind, and so I will now tell you how to train the body to become the servant of the mind, for the welfare of the body becomes of importance to all who seek to tread the path of Initiation, and to become the servants of the most high Gods. You cannot become receptive to the inflow of the spirit or tap the source of all knowledge, if you have a diseased body; therefore, it is necessary to understand the importance of the parts played by the body and mind in building a degree of perfection in those who seek Initiation. It is well known that a diseased mind makes a diseased body, because the mind—the vehicle of spirit—is able to control the blood-stream, the heart beats and the secretions of the different glands in the endocrine chain, and so we must find out how to become master of the mind, in order to escape the ills and irritations that seem to keep man from growing Godwards.

First, you should study your Horoscope, or ask some one who has knowledge to interpret it. Every Chela must have his birth map, then The Guru, understanding the law of the stars and knowing something of the vices, virtues, strength and weakness of his Chela, is able to guide him. Most Gurus have also a knowledge of herbs and minerals, and are able to direct the health of the Chela. To produce harmony in the cells, rhythmic breathing is taught, and much useful information in this connection is to be found in a book entitled " Fourteen lessons in Yoga Philosophy."

Naturally, thought plays a most important part in your well-being. You know that if you are over-tired you become irritable and depressed, and irritability and depression cause changes in the bloodstream. Depression would tend to bring about acidity, whilst irritation might be the cause of feverish conditions. Here again your Horoscope will help you to arrive at the cause of the irritation or depression, for you may find that certain transits or planetary configurations are affecting you adversely, and so you decide to cast out the feelings of irritation and to take more rest.

I understand that to-day you live in exceedingly difficult times. You have left behind you, as it were, the simple things of life and you have entered into the thought current of a mechanised age. There is within your minds the thought " hurry, hurry, hurry," and so you hurry through your work, your eating, your sleeping, and your recreation, thus burning up energy that should be stored for future use. The time is coming when there will be great changes in your world conditions and an enforced return to simpler ways of living and of thinking. If those of you desirous of treading the more interior way will study a few simple rules of right living, you can keep yourselves in good health, and a healthy body means a peaceful mind and the ability to generate feelings of harmony and brotherhood. By thus planning to transmute on a higher plane you live in more harmonious conditions and avoid the vicious circle of disease.

Once you begin to make a study of yourselves, you learn your capabilities and to what you can attain. Man must begin to realize that he has the power to transmute energy into forces that can work at a distance; that the energy he expends in worrying or perhaps running hither and thither to no purpose can, in certain cases, be used to better advantage if he sits in his home or office, and by the power of his thought draw to him the things that are his own. This is the law that governs all mankind. If a man is not intended by the Gods to amass wealth, although by his early endeavours he may make a fortune, it may be taken away from him later in life. But a man who realizes his God-given powers and wants only that which is his own, can use this force to attract it to him, whether it is wealth or plant, mineral, animal or human being; whatever it may be, he can cause it to flow into his very nature to where it manifests as a reality, thus transmuting the energy he would otherwise scatter so wastefully to his mental and physical undoing.

This is no fairy tale that I am trying to tell you; it is simply a matter of learning to reconstruct many of your ideas. Once you begin to believe in the law of re-birth, and to make a study of yourselves, you know your capabilities and to what you can attain. Those of you who have studied Astrology know perfectly well that you may be born at a date and hour that will take you to the very top of the mountain without any great effort, and yet under other planetary configurations you seem to climb two steps forward and slip three backwards. Once you find yourself in the scheme of things, and have reached a certain stage of spiritual growth, you will find that perfect harmony comes into your being; you will link up with Nature and the Devas, Angels, and other inhabitants of the elemental kingdom will obey your requests, will bring you their wealth, and the things that are rightfully yours will come to you for your use and enjoyment.

One of the reasons that you have been taught something of symbology and the law of the stars is that you might understand yourselves; because your destiny is written not only in the heavens, but in your head, your face, on the soles of your feet, in the palms of your hands, in the glance of your eye and in the sound of your voice. As you study your Horoscope you learn the strength and the weakness in your mental, moral and physical constitution, and so you know your lot in life. You know from whence you came and whither you are going. With this knowledge you can become the Governor of your body, and your brain, being healthy and well-balanced, is able to control the bloodstream and the various organs of the body, so that every particle of you will live in harmony, unity and love.

Disease of the body shows that there is disharmony in the mind; you may not be conscious of it; sometimes the inharmony causing the disease may be traced back for many years, perhaps to childhood days. It may be due to a fit of temper or petulance, or possibly a childish hurt or grievance at being misjudged. In such cases the mind doctor may be useful, for if you can get the mind to reveal its secrets you may be able to find the cause of the trouble and can assure the sub-conscious that the hurt is forgotten. Having thus torn out the source of the disease by its roots, the patient begins to live his life anew.

Many middle-aged people to-day are suffering from suppressions in youth. A part of the evil of your time is the result of a generation ago, when everything that was natural and beautiful was hidden away, and the mind was taught to regard it as foul, unclean and wholly destroying to the soul. To-day you are courageous and are teaching your children to regard all things pertaining to the body in a natural way, and so you are building for future generations a standard of healthier ways. You should teach your young ones to breathe correctly. From the moment they can make sounds, teach them to sing, because as you teach them to articulate sound, so are you teaching them rhythm and harmony. This brings about a feeling of joyousness and upliftment, and children respond like flowers to the Sun. Do not repress them in innocent amusements, but when you do not wish them to do certain things, always seek to explain to them the reason, and give them a reasonable answer to their questions so that you do not leave with them a sense of sin, darkness or terror. Have no false modesty. False modestry breeds disease of the generative organs. Having given you these few hints in connection with the upbringing of children, I must return to the older people and to something that is a curse of your times and a menace to your spiritual and psychic development, and that is the lack of control you have over the intestinal tract. Many of you continue day after day to accumulate poisons, and unless they be eliminated they become a breeding-ground for germs which not only poison the bloodstream but also corrupt the mind. I have noticed myself that people who have trouble with the intestinal tract become so imbued with thoughts of jealousy and suspicion that they make their lives dark and unhappy, and they take those thoughts into the lives of others.

Whilst dealing with the cleansing of the intestinal tract, we come to the use of water. Now water is a great cleanser, but it is often better to use it to clean the outside rather than the inside of the body, and here again you can be guided by your Horoscope. Those of you who come under earth signs should remember that too much water added to earth, makes mud. Therefore, people with planets in earthy signs should avoid drinking quantities of water. With a preponderence of fiery signs, it is advisable to be very careful in your choice of mineral waters so that you may avoid those containing iron or sulphur. When the airy signs are strong, it is good to take fruit juices mixed with water; and those who come strongly under watery signs may drink plenty of water, because it is their own element.

Sometimes a healer will tell his patient to drink plenty of water—two or three pints a day—without stopping to consider whether the person so advised has a body that will benefit from the absorbsion of large quantities of water. Some waters are impure; containing minerals they are injurious to certain signs, therefore it behoves the person who is told to drink quantities of water for the cleansing of the body to make quite sure that he belongs to a type that can do so with advantage.

Another thing that can be very injurious to some people is the washing out of the intestinal tract, and this is especially the case with people under the sign Virgo. Here I will add a few words of caution to those people born under the influence of Virgo. They are the greatest healers of any of the signs and have strong magnetic power, not only to heal themselves but to heal others also; they have however a weakness inasmuch as when ailing themselves, they like to try different mediums and different healers, and so often become the victim of their own desire for change as this frequent mixing of vibration retards their progress. To ensure good health, Virgo people have only to see that the bloodstream is kept pure. This they can do by avoiding criticism, mischief-making, their love of chatter, and by keeping themselves strictly to the highest attributes of the sign, which is maternal love and purity. Please do not think that I am being especially critical of Virgo people because each sign has its positive and negative qualities. We know, for instance, that Libra people are very prone to have trouble with the fluids of the body, therefore they should be very careful of the fluids they take and, above all things theyshould avoid stimulants of an alcoholic nature, because they inflame the bloodstream and set up inflammatory conditions. Taureans should avoid starchy foods; they should take foods that are watery and easy of digestion. Dairy foods are especially good for them. Gemini people should live as much as possible on fruits, especially fruits that grow on high trees. Those born under Cancer will find that they derive a great deal of nourishment and goodness from things that live in the sea.

A knowledge of colour and sound is also very necessary for those who are seeking to tread the more interior way, because colour plays a great part in promoting harmony of both mind and body. Again the birth map is helpful, because as the Moon by progression passes through the different Houses of the Horoscope, there comes almost at once a longing for various colours, and perhaps a desire to clothe onself in a particular colour or

have it in the home. This is due to the body crying out for the vibration that that particular colour
can give; therefore one should try to satisfy that
desire and not be held back by convention. If you
go to a country where there is a love of colour and
where colour is displayed, I am sure you will find
that the people are more joyful, more gay of heart,
and gloom and depression fly away before the
vibration of certain colours. Endeavour to present
the God-part of your nature in as bright and as
pleasing a manner as possible.

To those who are clair-audient, colour has
sound. I have spoken to you of the note B, which
note, if constantly sounded, brings into being
waves of perfect turquoise blue. If the note is stac-
cato, you will get little fleecy clouds of a very pale
blueish-white flitting across what seems to be a
blue sky, and if you harmonise this note of B into
chords and continue to play, you obtain a beautiful picture of youth, love and spring-time. If all
this can come from the harmonizing of the chord
of one note, think how much more harmony can
pervade the whole of your body for one whole day,
or even some few hours, when you give way to
your desire for a certain colour. It restores balance,
banishes fatigue, renews mental energy and re-
freshes and uplifts the whole body, because you
have responded to the spiritual urge to bathe the
body in the colour with which for the time being
the soul requires.

QUESTIONS

Q. I have the Sun in Leo. What would you recommend me to drink?

A. For the Sun in Leo, I should take the juices of all golden coloured fruits and add them to the water you drink.

Q. When you say fiery signs, do you mean a majority of the planets in fiery signs?

A. Well, I would consider a fiery ascendant of importance. After that, perhaps a predominance of planets in fiery signs.

Q. People who take Spa waters sometimes find that their health is improved for a short period only. Why is that?

A. When you go to a place and partake of the waters, you are in the thought current of people who regard the waters as health giving and your mind, being receptive, responds and you feel better. You come away and gradually the old conditions reassert themselves. It is not the waters that have brought relief so much as your receptivity to the thought current.

Q. Have bananas any special food value?

A. Bananas were brought to your world by the Angels of Venus, and so I should say we might consider they were ruled by Venus. They are good sparingly taken and with cream. Never mix your fruit and your vegetables at one meal, but you can mix fruit and cereals or fruit and dairy produce.

Q. You mentioned that depression caused acidity in the bloodstream. Would it be possible for acidity to be caused by a wrong colour vibration?

A. Shall we put it in this way, my son. Since a Saturnian influence brings about depresson, a person might have too much dark green or too much dark blue in the environment, and that would tend to bring about an excess of acid.

Q. Most of us have a certain number of meals a day at more or less conventional times. What do you consider the best time to eat?

A. Well, my son, I would say eat when you are hungry and not before, but I hear that to-day you have your meals at pre-arranged times and eat whether you are hungry or not, and so I would like to take you into an Egyptian household some six thousand years ago. It is hot, the air warm, and we sit in the court yard. We are expecting friends, and in response to our clapping of hands our servant-man brings two bowls of fruit and places them upon the table. He also brings two drinking vessels, jugs you would call them. In one there is a fermented drink that is made from honey, in the other there are fruit juices; and our banquet is laid. Presently our friends arrive, two at a time as a rule, and they sit around and help themselves to the fruit and drink whenever they feel the desire to do so, and we are very merry together.

We talk about many things, but we find our joy in the meeting rather than in the banquet provided although the fruit is sufficient to enable us to have friendly eating together, because it is realised that if a man eats in your house he cannot harm you without his evil intent coming back to himself.   Why must you have very heavy foods and drinks that stupify when you entertain your friends?   Why not have a party of friends and have your table laid with things that they can eat or drink, if and when they feel a desire to do so?   In my time it was considered vulgar to have a heavily laden table, but I have observed that it appears to be considered good taste in your time.   I do not know whether this is progression or retrogression—certainly retrogression so far as your bodies are concerned.

Q. Your way is better, I-Em-Hotep, but it is so difficult to find a way between wisdom and that which is conventional.

A. I think if a number of you had the courage to make a feast in your own home and invite your friends, calling it the Feast of Fruits or the Feast of Cereals, which ever you liked best.   You could provide something new and out of the ordinary, and in a short time you would find that your friends would be clamouring for an invitation to your house because they were not expected to eat at a fixed time or eat more than they wanted.

Q. Was the eating of meat common in Egypt in your time?

A. Only amongst the slaves. The standard diet of the people was vegetables, fruit, whole meal, dairy produce, mainly goat's milk, which by the way is much better than cow's milk.

Q. Do you advocate the eating of meat?

A. As man evolves he will gradually lose his desire for meat, but at the present stage of evolution most people in these latitudes require it. Study the Horoscope of a person and you may find that environment or inherited tendencies make a meat diet desirable; this is usually the case, but with certain people it may be necessary to make alterations, modifications or additions.

Q. Need fruit be eaten raw?

A. It is not necessary. When the Sun has moved away and the Earth is dark, there is nothing finer than the dried fruits you have stored away. They can be taken warm, and the liquid is good to drink. Some dried fruits have all the nourishing properties of the raw fruits.

Q. You said that Virgo people should not take large quantities of water. Does that apply to using water externally.

A. No, my daughter. It is good for Virgo people to immerse themselves in water because they assimilate the water necessary to their health through the pores of the skin. Moreover, when Virgo's are very tired, they will sometimes find it refreshing to bathe their feet in water. Remember, water signs, water internally; earth signs, water externally.

PRAYER

Oh Thou who art all love, we Thy children seek to draw near to Thee, we who are discarnate and these Thy children incarnate. Reveal Thyself to them as they seek earnestly for light. Help them to understand themselves; help them to find Thee within themselves; and we ask Thee that Thou wilt guide their footsteps along the paths of truth. Send unto each one of them an Angel Guardian to teach them the mastery of themselves. Bless their efforts to serve Thee; inspire them with Thy wisdom. Touch their eyes that they may see into Thy worlds, touch their ears that they may hear the voice of their Angelic Teachers, and touch their lips that every sound they utter may be a paean of praise and glory to Thy Holy Name.

Take them in, tired and weary souls seeking the homeward way. Let them have the power to perceive the light of love shed by the Mother-Aspect of Thee. Help them to feel the warmth and all-embracing love of Thy Christed Messenger, and let Thy peace descend upon them, Thy strength uphold them and Thy love enfold them in all their ways. Amen.

HERMETIC IDEALS

OUR subject to-night deals largely with the ideals of the Brotherhood of which I was a member and of which many of you are members. There are many Brotherhoods and many temples in which God is worshipped according to the type of mind that seeks Him, so please do not feel that I am trying to assume that my way of leading you along the interior path is the one and only way, but it is a way that has been tried, tested and proven, and those who come seeking along our pathway will attain if they but live and practise the ideals of the Brotherhood.

The Path of Initiation in the Hermetic Brotherhood is not an easy one, but one of constant endeavour, not only on the physical plane, but on the psychic, mental and spiritual planes as well. A A brother of the Hermetic Lodge realizes that he is a seven-, nine-, and twelve-fold being, and as soon as he has become a brother on the three-fold path, he is led by his instructors to where he becomes a brother of the seven-fold path and then the nine-fold, and later the twelve-fold, when he becomes a Crested Holder of the Christ Force.

The main ideal of the Hermetic Brotherhood is the desire that all shall work that they may come into at-one-ment or union with God. They know that in the secret chamber of the heart is a permanent atom, and it is a perfect likeness of themselves as God conceived them, and having come to the realization that there is a perfect spark of the divine within, the whole of the life is spent in trying to attain perfection. They learn obedience, charity, selflesssness, and are immune to praise or blame. They know that every person has a right to seek God and to express God in his or her own particular way. They realize that if they are drawn to a teacher or a group of any kind, that they are divinely led, and if the teaching does not appeal to them they do not criticise, but quietly leave in all charitable thought, seeking, ever seeking, until they find their own place.

And so you see, my friends, a brother of the Hermetic Lodge must be, above all things, sincere in his endeavours to find truth; kind, just and impersonal in all his dealings with his fellow men, ever striving to keep the ideal of perfection in front of him; living his life from the heart source, realizing that it is not what the lips are saying but what the mind is thinking and the heart is loving, that makes for perfection in seeking the way to God. To have love for all beings in your heart does not mean that you are sentimental; it does not mean that you must make a great show of demonstrating your affection; but it means that you have a sincere and impersonal love of God; and also that you would serve enemies and friends alike with the same impersonal kindness were they in need. It

also means that you realize your oneness with all
the kingdoms of the earth, and that just as God is
the wind and the water, the plant and the mineral,
so are you also a part of those kingdoms; and as
you advance in your studies, the inhabitants of the
various kingdoms know by the rate of your vibration, by the brightness of your astral or mental
bodies, that you are aware of their work and their
presence. As you are striving towards perfection,
they realize that you are for them a Master or a
Great One, and so they gather round you and seek
your aid. They can only judge of your growth by
your inner radiations; you can only be aware of
their presence by the height of your psychic and
spiritual perception; and so, as you make progress,
you begin to learn that you are no longer separated, but are one with the whole of the universe.
The wind, whether it be soft or stormy, has a message for you from the Lords of the Air; the water
may bring to you a message of peace, or it may
come in soft cleansing, healing, showers. It also
has a message for you from the Lords of Peace, or
Water. You may be filled with radiant energy or
filled with the desire of life, or filled with the rush
of power that makes you a magnetic healer; and
in this magnetism that flows through your veins,
energising and revivifying, you have a message
from the Lords of Flame; and as you seek to beautify your Earth, touching lovingly your flowers,
working patiently in your gardens, you are unifying yourselves with the Lords of the Earthly king-

H

doms; and serving them, and they in their turn
serve you. As you begin by service to harmonize
yourselves with these kingdoms, you touch their
higher secrets, you are able to feel the inrush of
force and the consciousness from the Great Devas
of the four kingdoms; thus you help them to carry
on their work of beautifying and of healing. What
a wonderful thought for those of you under air
signs, to identify yourselves with a Deva of the
air, with one who paints the clouds, who dresses
the ether with lovely sunsets. Think of the Devas
of the water, who arrange that their pools and lakes
shall reflect the work of their brothers of the air. As
you strive to understand these things, strive to
identify yourselves with those who work in those
kingdoms; then sunset, sunrise and their reflection
on water will have an additional meaning for you.

In this later civilized Age, it has been said that
in the beginning of time, people were nature wor-
shippers, but this is not wholly true. They adored
the Sun, the Moon and the Stars; they spoke of the
soft South winds, and many adored the rivers and
the places of trees, not because they worshipped
these elements as Gods, but because in their worship of the All-Father they made themselves one
with the inhabitants of these elements—the great
Devas of the forests and rivers, of the mountain tops
and the higher strata of air. As mankind in those
early days identified themselves with those Great
Devic workers for the Earth, so were they given a
finer revelation of what was God's plan regarding

the evolution of the Earth and the evolution of
humanity. Do not think that you must necessarily
die before you can partake of the wonder of the
spirit world. Try to think of the spirit world in
larger terms than as just a place where your beloved ones dwell. It is better to use the word spirit
in its wider sense to mean one without a physical
body, for your devas and your sprites, gnomes and
salamanders, are spirit also, and they can take you
to their kingdom and teach you much whilst you
are yet incarnate.

The Great Devas who govern the mineral kingdom know wherein are the secrets of the earth, and
under right conditions can help you to enrich the
earth. If you seek their aid you can help evolution,
because with the uncovering of the materials for
which men sweat and toil, there will be no need
for the greed of gold. Man will have time to reach
the heights of knowledge, to reach the unfoldment
of his spiritual self; to come into touch with the
Masters and those who are beyond the Masters;
and with increasing knowledge can eventually
overcome the change called death. And so man,
a spirit here and now, can become a co-worker with
the angels, because once he has reached a state of
consciousness that knows no limitation, he has
penetrated the Veil of Isis. You may remember
that it was said that Isis wore many veils and no
man could remove them and live. The fundamental meaning of that was that he who lifts the veil
of Isis, no longer lives as mortal man, but becomes

immortal, because he has the power to so change the atomic structure of his body in a way that will enable him to occupy it or not as he chooses.

It is not unusual to find that spiritualists are content to stay on the plane that brings them into touch with those they have loved. Now whilst this is perfectly legitimate, because it proves that love continues, yet there must also be those who desire to travel with their loved ones into the higher realms of the mental plane and to companion them there, for seekers on the path of initiation can learn to leave their bodies and travel at will into the realms of spirit, where they can companion their loved ones without waiting for the change called death. Therefore it behoves every Spiritualist who has proved the continuity of life, to rise higher than the psychic plane so that the mental plane may be contacted, rather than to develop on the psychic plane, where you may possibly see as through a glass darkly. If you develop your spiritual, mental and psychic powers simultaneously, the difference is so great that it may be likened to one living in bright daylight instead of being satisfied with twilight. At twilight everything loses its colour, but in daylight you see the reflection of all colours in the brightness of the Sun. Therefore, as you become more spiritual and are content to study all the things that give you knowledge of yourself, one by one the planes begin to open up before you. You will find your spiritual body becoming more radiant, your higher mind stimulated; the lower mental plane is able to reflect above and below and everything in the psychic plane becomes clearer.

And so we again return to the saying so often used by your Master, that if you seek first the kingdom of God, all things are added unto you. In seeking the kingdom of God one works from the highest point downwards, and things become clearer because you know the reason why. The Hermetic Brotherhood teaches its students first of all to understand themselves. It puts them through a more or less severe training that brings about a more rapid functioning of the various planes of mind. It teaches them to perceive that what is in themselves is in all men, and so they begin to learn a language that is Celestial. It teaches that man, in himself, is made in the counterpart of the Elohim, and the source of his origin is written all over him as well as the use he has made of his talents and whither he is going. It teaches him greater tolerance because he knows that a man, until he has learnt to rule his stars, is driven by destiny. He can learn that his health is a matter of perfect gland functioning, and that his mind has the power to make these glands function perfectly; so it all comes back to what a man thinks, so he is. Man in himself is the Governor of a Solar system, and this Solar system is within him. He can rule every cell of his being; he can become a conscious co-worker with the Angel world; he can identify himself with all that lives and moves, and as he realizes that he is a part of the universe, a Solar system in miniature, he begins to understand himself, and beginning to understand himself he is able to share with his less intelligent or less evolved brothers and sisters the knowledge he has gained, and together they can proceed along the path.

A brother of the Hermetic Lodge recognizes his unity with all systems of religion and all types of constructive thought. If you study the history of the great leaders of humanity, you will find that a a certain time in their life they began to study humanity; they visited different countries and studied different religions. They learned the law of the stars, the use of magnetism, the control of the mind, and as they gathered all this knowledge, they taught their pupils according to their receptivity.

The time is now ripe for a new religion, and the new religion will be one of the mind as well as of the heart. Hitherto religion generally has been much too emotional in one form or another, with the result that your religions have broken up, so to speak, into many pieces; but if in the future you build as a foundation one religion recognizing the needs of all, then you have as in the olden days one head source but many grades or schools. When this system is established on your Earth, you will find that greater peace and harmony will prevail, because when you are all of one brotherhood or one religion, and although you may see it from a different point of view according to your status in evolution, and your main idea is for progress, and you begin to realize that no one can retard your growth but yourself, no one can raise you from poverty or sickness but yourself, and so you begin to use your thought forces to bring you nearer to God. You begin a new system of education, and you begin to learn the way of power. And so the ideals of the Hermetic Schools are, union with God, union with man, courage and faith; tolerance, love, and impersonality. As the Hermetic brothers strive to live these things, so the key of knowledge is given to them and they become co-workers with the great Hermes, who was a son of God.

To-night, I have to some extent gone over old ground, but it may help you to understand why the talks have continued. Remember, however, I can only point the way, I can only help you to a little understanding of these things—the rest lies with you.

QUESTIONS

Q. I-Em-Hotep, you have told us to think with the heart and not only with the mind. How can we blend the two?

A. My daughter, if you think only with your mind, you develop a keen intellect that lacks love or compassion, therefore you must add another ingredient and think with the heart also.

Q. What is it that causes a soul to seek the things of the spirit?

A. Sometimes it is a force stronger than yourself. It is the inner urge of the spirit that recognizes links with the past. Consider my relationship with you. I do not come here with my eyes closed. I know my own by their light and the thought forces they carry. Many of you will cling to me, others will drift away. We meet here week after week and we cannot be held in the Aura of God, and in the Aura of the Great Ones, without deriving mutual benefit. Some of you will carry memories of these talks for many days.

Q. A friend of mine has been told that he has a most lovely and brilliant aura. Should he believe that statement?

A. I do not know your friend, but, speaking generally, I should say beware of flattery. If you are told that your aura shines with magnificent colouring, instead of being pleased with yourself, search within. Examine carefully what you have done by word, thought or deed that your aura should have a beautiful iridescence. What have you done for humanity that enables you to become a useful servant of the Great Ones? You must achieve something tangible, and when you have done this, your emanation will glow with luminosity.

Q. How can a pupil make his mind sufficiently sensitive to receive the inspiration of the Teacher or Guru?

A. You must prepare yourself and to do this you

must have a certain amount of knowledge, for
when there is sufficient knowledge in the conscious mind, the higher mind or inspirational
force can flow down more easily into the conscious mind. My own instrument—some time
ago, before she was aware of me in the sense
she is now—only knew me as some one who
gave her thoughts. She was told to speak, and
she asked "How can I speak without inspiration?" I now give you the same answer that I
gave her : "He who would receive inspiration
must be prepared to do without it and always
say to himself—I speak not myself but am
guided by the spirit within."

Q. In the Egyptian Book of the Dead there is a
picture of the soul being weighed in the Judgment Hall of Osiris, and when I meditated upon
this picture, it occurred to me that a reflection of
that judgment might be found in the experiences of those who are treading the path of the
aspirant?

A. There comes a period in the life of every Initiate when there is a weighing of the soul. It
comes during the "Illumination," a period
when the soul must descend into the darkness
before it awakens to the new life. Preceding
this Supreme Initiation, there is the preparation, the forty days fasting; for forty days you
are in the wilderness and then the soul is released by the Hierophant and soars into the
Ethereal Realms, meeting the Great Initiator,

who tells the soul why it has come such a long and tiresome journey. By the end of the third day, it knows the Astral World and the higher strata of the Spiritual Worlds. It is during those three days that you are given the secret name of power; it is through the experience gained that you are able to tell the Initiate from the self-styled Initiate. Your inner eyes are opened and you know the real from the false. The soul has been baptised with spirit; it is given a new name and it returns to Earth and commences its work as a Teacher of Wisdom, that it may serve the Great Ones. It becomes one of a group known as the Illuminati. Every school that teaches the things of the spirit has its own system of Initiation according to its grade and according to the Neophites. The lesser Initiates, when they have done the necessary work and passed their tests, become fitted to receive the Supreme Illumination. In my day we had in our temples a part that was named the Court of the Sacred Sleep. The Sarcophagus in your Great Pyramid was where the Initiate was laid for His three days' sleep and Illumination.

Q. Does this Illumination take place to-day?

A. I have known business men who study along these lines to arrange for their Illumination during their yearly vacation. It is a test of endurance—forty days of fasting—and it needs a great deal of care to keep balance of mind and health of body   It cannot be done without a teacher.   To learn the outer things gives you a great deal of wisdom, which blended with the love of God embedded in your heart, enables you to pass from one grade to another almost imperceptibly.

Q. Can this be done in one incarnation?

A. Not from the very first, my daughter.   I have told you that it takes three incarnations.   There is no real Initiation on the spirit planes without an outer manifestation.   What is written in your Horoscope?   There you will find the mundane, spiritual and psychic interpretations, and in nearly all schools which are on the right lines, in whatever country you search, the same procedure takes place.   You are not received on your own recommendation but by what your stars show you to be.   You may have aspirations, but aspirations are not always accepted; therefore you are received and you are led just as far as your Horoscope shows you are capable of being led.   Your wealth or position are of no moment to a genuine teacher, and you are dealt with quite impersonally.   The time is coming when this relationship will be better understood.

Q. Does the Horoscope show the most suitable type of teacher?

A. The Horoscope shows the type of teacher suitable for the aspirant, but you must understand that the Hierophant, of any school, is a fit teacher for any one on any plane.

Q. From what you have said, I gather it is necessary to have a teacher in the flesh?

A. A teacher incarnate in the flesh is necessary at certain stages.

Q. Would a Rosicrucian belong to the Great White Lodge ?

A. The Great White Brotherhood has existed since time began. It is composed of Angels and Men made perfect. They have their grades, officers and government, and naturally. this great Brotherhood has different Lodges; the Rosicrucian is one, just as the Hermetic is another. The Rosicrucians were founded a few hundred years ago; the Hermetic Lodge was founded some thousands of years ago. The fundamental ideals are the same. The founder of the Rosicrucians was an Illuminati who taught esoteric thought at the time in which he lived. He was a very great man. Swedenborg was an Illuminati, Steiner another; each teaching something of the same, each being an Illuminati who taught and drew certain types around him. just. as to-day you have your guides and your teachers who draw around them the people who are best suited for their teaching; no one is greater than another, and all are different steps. Leadbeater was also an Illuminati, but he was first led along the path by coming into touch, I believe, with Blavatsky. Blavatsky and Anna Kingsford were both '' Illuminati ''

—they were the heralds of the dawn of the Aquarian Age. You see those two great women were the ears unto God, and the men they gathered around them were able to express their words for the good of humanity; but because they were the holders of the wisdom and the ear unto God, to them must the Honour be given.

Q. I have been trying to understand a passage in " Light on the Path." It is this : " No man is your enemy, no man is your friend, all alike are your teachers," and that seems a hard thing?

A. No, because just as I said, you are inclined to be sentimental; if you love impersonally, you do not expect friendship and you do not feel criticism. No man is your friend because you are the friend of all kingdoms. No man is your friend because you are the friend of all. You do not regard these things in a personal way.

Q. But when one has people who sacrifice themselves to serve, with no idea of personal gain or reward, not even desiring one's love, it seems hard not to regard them as friends.

A. You may regard them in the physical sense as friends, but not in the spiritual sense. You see, in treading the interior pathway you cut out the personal sense of things. I will put it to you in another way : if you are a child of God, then you are brother and sister to all humanity. If a brother, seeking to love God, seeking to express his love for God, finds that there is one in need, through no fault of his own, then does he supply that need not from a sense of friendship, but from a sense of Sonship with God. You see it is identifying yourself with the Father.

PRAYER

Oh Thou eternal, all-wise, all-loving Mother! We, Thy children, draw near to Thee, incarnate and discarnate, seeking Thy wisdom. Fill the minds of these Thy children with peace; fill their hearts with love, fill their minds with the desire to serve Thee. Let Thy divine energy flow through them, raising them up until they draw near. Help them to the realization that Thou art within them; and from Thy breast flow ever in continual streams their food and their sustenance.

All-wise and tender, loving Father, let Thy power fill these Thy children. Let them feel that they are indeed Thine own, and that all their requirements shall be supplied by Thee.

Now let Thy peace descend upon us until it fills the whole of the world, and harmony prevails.

Amen.

THE HERMETIC MYSTERIES

TO-NIGHT I propose to talk to you about the Hermetic Mysteries, which in the early days of Egypt were known as the Mysteries of Thoth, but at a much later period they were known as the Mysteries of Hermes, and this name has survived even to this day.

When Egypt was young, those who were concerned with the destiny of the race left behind them records of the Teaching for the use of future races. Much of this teaching had to be clothed in terms of symbology, and that necessitated a system of grading suitable to the receptivity of the group or class where the Teaching was given. Each member of a grade wore the Symbol of its Ray of God, and was given a name symbolizing a representative of God.

Most of you know that Egypt has been proclaimed as the land of many Gods, and if you follow carefully you will see how this tradition arose. The early Egyptian chose His representative of God and worshipped Him in the sense that he revered Him. He did not worship Him as God, but regarded Him as an intermediary between the Great All-Father and himself in much the same way as you to-day look upon certain Holy Men as Saints.

In the early days of Temple Life we had three types of Priests. Those of the highest grade came under the Ray of Osiris; those who had reached the second grade were called the Priests of Isis, and those of the third grade the Priests of Horus. We had also, Priests of Thoth, Set, Amen, and so on throughout the whole calendar of Egyptian Deities. The Priests were the recipients of much reverence, and so strong has been the esteem and love felt by the erstwhile student for his Priest, that a link has been forged in the ethereal world. And so to-day the Priests have returned to those who loved them in the far distant past.

Much of the teaching pertaining to the Inner Mysteries was connected with the symbolism of the signs of the Zodiac. For instance, the Sun was the symbol of Osiris—the Eye of the Gods. The Moon was Isis, or in another aspect Nephtys, and it also symbolized the Celestial Ship of the North. The infant Horus was represented by Sirius. Many of you know that Hermes or Thoth was the Ibis-headed God, and was known as the Scribe or the Bearer of Messages between the celestial kingdoms, and you may know that there were other Deities worshipped and revered amongst the ancient ones.

Our Temple was usually situated in the centre of the village or town, and was the place where all the treasures of the town and the people were kept. In times of famine the people went to the Temple; in times of illness to the Temple also;

and when the Great Temple Festival was held, there would be a Play similar to what you in your day would call the Play of the Nativity. By means of such a Play or other pictorial representation we taught the common people, that is those of the labouring class and those who were uneducated. For instance, just as at Christmas time you have in some of your Churches the representation of the Child in the cradle, the Holy Mother, the Wise Men and the animals, so did we use that method to enable the ignorant and the untutored to hold in their minds the picture form of the symbolism of our religions.

In those days only the Priests could read and write, and only they held the Sacred Mysteries. Into their hands were given the guidance and destiny of the race, and they gave the whole of their lives to the study of the heavens, to the study of healing, and to the study of ruling and helping the people to evolve to a higher state of consciousness. It would be of no use to tell an untutored mind that to-day was the beginning of a new round of re-births, but if you could give him some picture form of a Glorified Being, and tell him that if he emulates the life of that Glorified Being, it would mean a step forward in evolution; or you would explain to him that to do good deeds, to speak kind words, to share with his neighbour, and to live in the Great Light of the All-Father, would be for him to have a safe passage in the underworld and be

I

able to meet the Ibis-headed One and receive good judgment.

From this pictorial representation of the truths of the religious life, I understand there has grown up many myths and legends, many misconceptions of our early ways of living, and yet as I wander amongst you to-day I find that you have your Temples and you teach unthinking, unevolved people symbology, which under other names is similar to the symbology of Egypt. In one of the talks received you were given the exercise of I. A. O.*. Isis, Apophis, Osiris. It was the old, old ritual of drawing down the Solar and Lunar forces to re-awaken and cleanse and energise your bodies—the Solar force to purify your atoms and the lunar force to awaken the psychic power. Is is not strange that after several thousand years you should be receiving the same teaching under another name? And is it not strange that you were taught to image the force in your Master Jesus taught to image from your Master Jesus the force coming up through the body, ascending around and down, just as we in ancient Egypt told our students to imagine the arisen Horus, or the Son of the Sun? And so throughout all ages the same symbolism and the same teaching prevails. We did not worship idols, but we gave to the untutored ones an image by which in their busy lives, unlettered, untaught, they could concentrate on something that would raise them to a higher state of consciousness.

* See Appendix.—Ed.

Then on their sacred days, their days of rest, there came into the lives of those toilers, something of joy and of beauty—the beginning of ritual, the perfumes of the incense, the colours of the priestly robes, the burning of the sacred candle and oil, the sacred Lotus, and the images of the Divine Osiris, Isis and Horus. And it remained in the minds of these people and built up a simple faith that they tried so hard to live up to. Surely their simple faith and their understanding of the love force behind its symbols has brought man to a higher state of evolution, to where he can think and reason for himself. He is then able to decide whether he will continue in the same old way or whether he will try to get to the source of all knowledge.

State religion or man organized religions must ever be for the untutored or unenlightened members of the race, because there are in humanity people of all grades to be provided for. There are the once born, and there are the twice born. The once born would not understand unless they had the symbols to follow, whilst the twice born are those who have outgrown symbols and want to reach the meaning behind it. For all grades of people there is the ever-shining light. In the olden days we had, as I believe you have to-day, a very tall candle always placed in the midst of our altar. This symbolized the Eternal Light, because, ever since this world came into being there has been the Eternal Light from on high to guide and help humanity.

When man has become enlightened, when he

begins to understand that the heavens are God's book to him and he studies celestial symbolism, and he realizes that all the pictorial representations of the past concerning religion are but symbols, and so as he begins to understand his kinship with the Architect of the Universe, he puts away, as it were, the toys of religion, and he begins to climb the homeword way. No more is he immersed in matter, no more does he seem to bend his head playing with these toys of early man, but raising his head till it reaches the stars, he looks upright and bravely forward—a man seeking God. Such a man realizes that he can become as God, and he is no more concerned with any religion but that which lies between him and He who created him. As man comes to this realization, he builds within his heart centre an altar to the Unknown God; an altar to the Unnameable God, and He worships Him in spirit and in the sacred innermost chamber. As he worships Him, and raises his thoughts to Him, he begins to hear in the silence of his mind, he begins to hear as he kneels before the altar in that innermost chamber of himself, and in time there comes a voice that utters a sacred syllable. He has become enlightened. He has become one who some day shall know the whole name of God. The God that is not worshipped in any Temple, the God that is beyond all Gods, the God who is the Creator and Architect of the whole universe, the Lord of many Suns, the Creator of untold millions of worlds, the Overlord of many Gods. When man awakens to this realization, he becomes in mind serene, he becomes filled with power and peace; he knows that all is well within him. Gone is the lust of power, gone is the desire for material gain, gone is the desire for all the smallness and pettiness that belongs to the men of the world, and he feels himself raised up and glorified in this unknown power that emanates from the Creator of all.

Behind the mysteries, there was always the reaching out to this Unknown Force. As the Priests began to make headway in their studies and in their understanding, so they passed from grade to grade, until finally they came to that last grade in which their soul was set free that it might wander in the underworld and the overworld, seeking union with God the Creator. And when the Priest returned, having come into touch with the Force of the Creator, he became enlightened and lived only for the good of the whole. Many, many are there even to-day, who have returned and who remember that past Illumination, who remember their strivings. They give themselves to practises that will enable them to remember their past training, for it is imprinted upon them that they are those who have tasted of the Flowers of the Lotus. Deep down in their minds is the knowledge that they garnered in long past incarnations, and it rises up as each New Age comes round, and the great Masters who return to your Earth as the Christs, find these faithful ones seeking to work with them for the service of mankind. There can be no higher desire in the heart of man, woman or child, than to yield the whole of the self in full consciousness and full faith to the service of the Unknown God, realizing that the Sun is the Father and the Moon the Mother, that he can be as one born of both, inhabiting a body composed of atoms of the earth, knowing that he—realizing the whole of his divine inheritance—will have the power to bring to him that which he has earned the right to receive. God the Creator never withholds from His faithful servants their wages, but He does not pay the unfaithful and those concerned only with their own business. Faithful and just is He to pay the wages of those who serve Him and render themselves to Him for His service.

Many of you, day after day, complain of the hardness of your fate. You may suffer from poor health or feel the lack of material things, or again you may hold yourself ready for service and wonder why opportunities are withheld. To those I would say : study the laws of re-incarnation, look into your own nature and find out the reason. What is your motive in offering yourself? Is the motive one of self-aggrandisement? Does self-will come into it? Are you content to give up all and follow that higher light—your intuition? Or do you say " If God gives unto me, I will do so and so?" If you feel ill in body, have you enough faith to find out the reason and heal yourself of your illness? A body that is ill may be compared to a garden full of weeds, and you take medicine even as you would pour weed-killer over your garden, resulting perhaps in a temporary relief from pain, but if the roots are not pulled out and the cause ascertained, a similar pain may occur in another part of the body.

Do you suffer from poverty, or what you think is poverty? Would you be selfless in the use of any wealth that God might make you the warden of? By this I do not mean that you should not save for your family; even the beasts of the field hunt for their young : that is the call of nature. But as you gather you must remember that you gather in for God, and as you gather in wealth, using it for the furtherance of God's work on the Earth plane, then is good interest added unto you.

In the early days of Egypt, it was the custom to have a Temple Treasury, and into this rich and poor gave certain tithes, so that if war came upon the land, it was the Temple Treasury that provided that which was necessary. If famine came upon the land it was the Temple Treasury that again provided relief. The Temples were also the guardians of the wealth of the kings. Later in your history, the Priests misused their power, and to-day you have but the shadow of what religion was once meant to be.

Reflection upon God in His-Her many aspects should bring about the realization—according to his status and education—of the responsibilities of the individual. If you realize these things, and live up to the law of God, then shall evolution proceed apace. But to-day you are in the balance, and men and women who think, must realize their responsibilities, or the wheel must turn again. I am confident myself that there are men and women whose intuitions are so well-developed that they could interest others, and so help to develop the intuitions of others; and if you are fearless and strong in your beliefs, if you take the trouble to study and are able to talk intelligently concerning your beliefs, then you gain a certain amount of respect and become the fore-runners of a new dispensation, thus preparing the way for the Saviour of all.

In a school of this kind it would be quite easy for you amongst yourselves to make a tableau, or to make a play showing some Divine outpouring. That would teach your people, because they would see with the eye and hear with the ear, and so by the picturisation of Divine truths, such truths would sink deeper into the heart and remain longer in the mind, than if you just confined yourself to talking about these things.

Do not be afraid to talk of the book of the heavens. Do not be afraid to talk of the Great Ones who walk amongst the stars. And if in your world at the present moment there are charlatans, and there are those who use the Divine Science for the amusement of the foolish, be strong and courageous, and make it known that they who prostitute the Divine Science are not of your Ray. And as you go on day after day striving to understand.

trying to learn more, so will more light be given to you, because on my side, coming close to your world, there are a great many sages, a great many ancient priests who are highly evolved, and they are looking for instruments to impress and use, that the ancient wisdom shall be restored. He who has knowledge can heal the sick, can bring into manifestation all things needful for the welfare of mankind, and at the dawning of this Age, we who watch over you shall renew your strength and bring all things to your remembrance, that you may go forward with greater courage. So learn to read a map of the heavens, and you will see, as you quote glibly your signs of the Zodiac, how those signs are made up of different constellations of stars, and in nearly every constellation there is a great Sun which is the abode of the Spirit of that sign. And so instead of saying that Mars is the ruler of Scorpio, you will find out the fixed star in the constellation of Scorpio is in reality a bright and brilliant Sun. In this Sun resides the Master Builder, the God, the Guardian Spirit of all those who are born on that Ray. This celestial astrology contains much that is of greater interest than anything you can find in mundane Astrology. It helps you to an understanding of the Divine purpose behind all things.

An interesting example of what I have just been telling you is to be found in the great Step Pyramids. Each step had upon it a symbol, and this symbol was an adoration to one of the Gods who governed a constellation. It has been thought, and is told in exoteric circles, that each step is given to a ruler of a sign, but it was really given to the ruler of a constellation. You see that is slightly different. On the top of the Pyramid there was the space for the Table of Remembrance, and here the Feast of Remembrance was held according to which star or constellation the Pyramid was builded. Your great Pyramid, you call it, was builded to the honour and glory of the Great Divine Lord who dwells in Sirius, and at certain times of the year, when Sirus came right over the top, then was the Feast of Remembrance partaken of by His Priests. And you know, because you have been told many times, that the Sphinx indicates the four fixed signs. It may interest you to learn that whenever the Horoscope of the World is in fixed signs, it is a time of peace and a time of spiritual awakening. That again is another of the symbolical meanings of the cross. The cross means peace attained, and in the World Horoscope a fixed cross stands for attainment. A mutable cross is a time of great struggle; a cardinal cross a time of many changes.

QUESTIONS

Q. In comparing the position of the Temple in the life of the people of Egypt with the position of our Temple to-day, it has occurred to me that the difference may be explained to some extent by the fact that in Ancient Egypt the Priests were vasly better educated, had greater knowledge and more highly developed faculties. Our Priests of to-day may be educated, but so also are many people outside the Priesthood. Therefore the priests do not stand unique as a separate class, as they did in Egypt. Has that anything to do with it?

A. No, my son; perhaps I have not made my meaning clear. I was trying to compare the difference in this way: that because there are outside your priestly class many people of intelligence and education, they should realize their responsibility and not be content to take religion as presented by the Priests of to-day. They should perceive that whilst the Priests of to-day may be, as you say, highly educated—but in this I disagree although I think they may be highly trained—yet they are only educated along one or two lines. They do not understand the Celestial Science. They may understand material science, but they have never got beyond the third dimension, whereas the old-time priest was a scientist on all planes of consciousness. At the same time our Priests were hampered more than your Priests of to-day, because outside our priestly circles and the nobility, the people generally had not the standard of education that is to be found in your land to-day, and so our people could only be taught by simple symbols. But to-day, I

notice that from your labouring class upwards,
there is religion for all, but your Priests do not
realize their responsibilities, they do not help
the people to think for themselves, to develop
their intuitive qualities, and the Inner Light.

Q. Although the truth of Astrology is accepted by
many well-educated people it is not easy to
persuade people of scientific attainments to investigate the subject?

A. It would be different if the majority of educated
people insisted upon the investigation of your
Celestial Science in the same way as they do
other matters. Am I not right in thinking that
you have in your universities special facilities
for the investigation of certain sciences, thereby
wasting much time and money, whereas if
there were facilities for the investigation of the
Celestial Science, you would find that you
would have the key to other Sciences? You see
your medical men to-day do much research work
and do much good. I must not cast reflections
because I am of their brotherhood, but I remember what took place thousands of years
ago. We developed the Inner Intution, we
developed the Inner Sight, that we might
understand the ills of the body. We practised
dentistry, we understood the circulation of the
blood, we were familiar with many things that
are not well known to-day. Sometimes, when
excavating in my beloved land, you make discoveries that show that thousands of years ago

these things were known and practised, whereas, if you had tried to develop your Inner Mind,
all these things and many more would be
known to you. You seem to me to go such a
long way round in these matters.

Q. Have we become steeped too deeply in material
matters?

A. My child, I would not say that, so much as that
you have wrong values. You have let yourselves be governed by racial thought until it
has shut out, generation after generation, the
Divine Light, and you are still allowing this to
go on. I cannot help thinking that if the study
of Celestial Science was encouraged, you
would make greater strides towards perfection.

Q. With regard to the study of Celestial Science,
where shall we find our teachers?

A. It is probable that amongst your highly educated Priests there would be some who had the
power of contacting the Celestial Realms. Do
you not know that your Roman Catholic
Church takes good care that certain of its
Priests shall investigate Psychic Science and
Occult Science? They have more knowledge
than the Priests of other so-called Christian
Churches, and this knowledge they keep to
themselves. Now as long as this is allowed to
go on, and as long as they regard other religions as unevolved and inferior to their own,
they are retarding the growth of their members.

Q. Will the Roman Catholic Church change in the

course of time?

A. Not until people demand that it shall change. The move must come from outside the church.

Q. The doctrine of infallibility does not help matters?

A. Have they not built up their religion on the old regime, and do they not draw people to them who are content to receive what they are taught without bothering to find out for themselves? If they do find out for themselves they may be excommunicated, and to the ignorant Catholic that is being debarred from Heaven. Yet some of your Catholics believe they are highly trained, highly educated and highly intelligent. Until man's intuition awakens and the Divine Serpent Force raises its head, man is not aware of the fourth dimension. Until man realizes that he has powers hidden within him and that study can bring them into manifestation, he is only partly educated. An evolved person is not held by any creeds. He realizes that no man is his master or dictator, but that he is a law unto himself because he is the son of the Living God. You see you have raised for yourselves in these later days, false Gods. You worship what you term intellect and you worship money. As I come near to your world I meet men whom you consider brilliant in the world of letters, but apart from their own particular knowledge, they are as babes, and it is sometimes amusing to watch the trend of their mind. They have developed along one line of intelligence and consider as fools or uneducated those who do not agree with them, not realizing that there are many strata of mind upon which they might become perfected.

Q. In dealing with the symbolism of the Step Pyramids, would you say that the number of the steps indicate a definite type of Pyramid?

A. The number of steps indicated the grade of the Priest of that particular temple.

Q. Would it be possible to have a step Pyramid which had twenty-three steps and a platform at the top?

A. Of course. At the apex of the Pyramid you would find your table raised on a platform, which would constitute the twenty-fourth step. You will find it interesting to note the number of stars in a constellation that seem chained to the fixed star of the constellation. You will then begin to derive something of the sacred symbology of number in relation to it. Also, the steps of the Pyramid will give you some indication as to what constellation it represented.

Q. Does not the fixed star of a constellation always represent the highest good?

A. That is so, my daughter.

Q. Even though we sometimes ascribe to them what we term malefic influence?

A. You might just as well say that when a malefic

influence is released when a mother chatises a child to prevent it harming itself. A star of the heaven world is not malefic in the true sense of the word. It is only man's reaction to its influence that makes it benefic or malefic. You see—perhaps I can put it to you this way— you pass through the gate of a constellation and you are born into a certain sign. Because of this, you are for that incarnation under the protection and guidance of the great Lord of the particular constellation. You may receive afflictions—opposition from other vibrations. That is only to test. strengthen and give the spirit courage and endurance to progress and learn the lessons of that constellation. Try to meditate a little on those fixed stars. Try to get into touch with the Lord of a sign.

Q. In the case of those who are born in Cancer, the ruler is the Moon. Well then, if the Lord of that constellation is a fixed star, would it work through the Moon on to the sign?

A. No, it is three-fold, the sign, the Moon and the star. You see, my son, I am trying to teach you a little of celestial astrology, and to do that you must forget the mundane presentation. I am dealing with the constellation in which you have incarnated. The constellation of Cancer and not the sign of Cancer, and it is well for you to study the constellation of Cancer. You see, you have a kinship with every star in the constellation of Cancer. I trust that those of you who are studying the stars will find this little bit of Celestial Astrology interesting, and that it will stimulate you to make further research.

Q. In applying that to an individual Horoscope, would you take the constellation rising, or the one in which the Sun appears to be?

A. No, my daughter, the constellation rising, because the constellation rising is the gateway through which the spirit has chosen to manifest. The Sun, shall we say in Taurus, has gained experience in the constellation of Taurus. It has gone through all the stars that make up that constellation.

Q. Would it be right to look upon every degree as a star which has a definite lesson to teach?

A. No, my son, you will not find that there are thirty stars in some constellations. In the triangle there are only three. No, no, you must not seek to tabulate in earth terms the celestial signs. You can only tabulate in celestial terms.

PRAYER

Oh Thou who art the Architect of the Universe, inspire our minds, and let Thy wisdom dwell within our hearts, for we Thy children of Earth and Spirit bow down before Thee in adoration. We worship Thee, we love Thee.

Oh Thou who are our Mother, take us in Thine arms and whisper in our ears the words of our Father God, that we may become Thy messengers,

J

carrying the good tidings of peace and joy into the world.

Accept the offering of these Thy children that they make at Thy knee, seeking the holy wisdom, seeking the sacred doctrines of the ancient ones. Enlighten them in all their ways. Help them to the realization of their own inherent powers. Help them to the realization that they are Thine own. Thou has heard their call for help throughout all the spheres; so, oh Holy Mother, let Thy words of wisdom fall upon their minds like healing rain.

Oh Thou who art the Father of all living, inspire them with Thy Holy Word, and let it vibrate through every cell of their being, giving unto them renewed life and regeneration. And we ask Thee too, that Thou would so open up every centre of their being, that it may be as a chalice filled with Thy Holy Spirit.

Let each one here be a torchbearer of peace and love in the outer world. Cleanse their bodies of all inharmony and disease. Cleanse their minds from all thoughts that are harmful, and join them together in the bonds of brotherhood and love that all may be one in Thee. Help them by a vision of Thy most sacred Heart, that they may find that in that Heart of Thine, the heart-beats of the universe.

Oh Mother most adorable, take us in. In all the realms of the spirit let Thy Name be adored. In all quarters of the Earth let the Earth re-echo Thy holiness. This is our prayer to Thee. We will wait to receive Thy Holy Mercy and Spirit. Amen.

DEVIC INITIATION

TO-NIGHT I touch the fringe of a vast subject—that of Devic Initiation. Many of you are beginning to understand something about the elemental kingdoms, and also that the Devas stand in the same relation to the inhabitants of the elemental kingdoms as the Masters do to humanity. So when we speak of a Deva, we are speaking of a being who is of the higher grade of the Angelic Kingdoms. The Devas are the Lords of the ethereal worlds, and their work is mainly concerned with the formation, the governing and the direction of all forms of nature, and the lower inhabitants of the elemental kingdoms work under their direction.

These Bright Beings who inhabit the ethereal realms are drawn to man, and you hear of them inspiring and directing great artists and musicians, stimulating the imagination and the thought currents of those who strive to unfold in man a love of the beautiful. Throughout the Ages you have had your inspired artists, poets, and musicians, and they have had the guidance or inspiration of one of these Devic Beings. So when man begins to respond in his highest vehicle to a love of beauty and tries to express his thoughts in sound or tries, however dimly, to beautify his surroundings, he comes into touch with the thought current of a

Deva.

The Devas stand at the head of the elemental race. There are Great Devas at the head of the Fiery Kingdoms, but these are not to be confused with the Lords of Flame. There are also Great Devas standing at the head of the watery kingdoms, the earthly kingdoms and the airy kingdoms; and the elemental beings serve them and carry to and fro upon the Earth, the messages of these Great Angels as they seek to inspire men towards beauty.

Your historians have told you something of the period when Greece was the centre of art and beauty, and at that particular time the Devic Kingdom had centred the whole of its force in the hope that it might help forward evolution by inspiring within mankind a love of the beautiful; but, unfortunately, Greece fell into a state of decadence and only during the last twenty years have the Devas again been able to come into touch with mankind. To-day man is throwing off the cloak of convention and receiving inspiration for the expression of colour and sound. In his surroundings he tries to portray more beautiful colours. He strives to express the thoughts of the Devic Kingdom in his garden, his home and his clothing.

You have been taught that colour plays a prominent part in health and well being, and that your physical body comes largely under the direction of these Angelic Beings. It is they who help in its formation and in moulding its contour. It is they who inspire the desire for beauty, so whenever there comes into your mind a desire to beautify the person, to beautify your surroundings and to have beautiful colours around you, try to give way to that desire, and try to understand that you are being influenced by one of these Angels of Beauty. If you open yourself to their call, your mind will be flooded with beautiful thoughts; with beautiful pictures; and you will have the power given to you to create beautiful works.

In the Spiritualist Movement, and very often outside it, you have many people who speak of being inspired by great artists, and who have an ability to do inspirational, or what they term automatic, painting or drawing. I hope I shall not disturb you if I tell you that very often the person using the name of an artist is really a servant of the Devic Kingdom who tries through the chosen medium, to create something of the beauty of the ethereal worlds. These Beings are especiallly drawn to those who have airy signs predominating, and they love to inspire their minds to execute their thoughts in pale and beautiful colourings. They also inspire them during their meditations with beautiful cloud-like pictures, although sometimes hazy and hard to catch, therefore, it behoves those who feel drawn to paint or draw or do any kind of work that will express colour or sound, to reach out and make it known in the Devic Kingdom that they are conscious of the drawing near of the inspirer. As man awakens more and more to an understanding of beauty in art, so will he feel himself lifted up into other dimensions. He will find that contact with these Bright Beings will bring ease of mind, beauty of body, and the power of inspiration in colour or sound. And as man gives way to the impinging of their contact upon his aura, so will your world begin to express itself in a very much more beautiful form of art. During the last twenty years it might appear as though the Devas in drawing nearer have created in the minds of some men that which is ugly; but, in their endeavours to draw nearer to the human family, they have had to use any mind that was receptive, and the outcome of the ugly in art has had the effect of making certain minds more receptive to the inflow of the beautiful. During the next generation you will see a return to the days when art in all its forms was considered one of the greatest assets in the education of humanity.

If these Great Beings come to you, do not mistake them for guides from a very high plane or a very high sphere. Try to understand that they are of a different evolution although a parallel one, and that they are used by the Angels of Beauty coming from Venus to transmute all that is lustful, all that is of the lower passions, into something that is beautiful and creative. It is the custom I know to consider that every contact made with the spiritual realms must be with a discarnate human being, but

as we strive to come into contact with other planes
of consciousness, we must make ourselves receptive and review the idea that there are parallel
evolutions.   And as we realize our own possibilities whilst incarnate in matter to contact these
ethereal realms, so shall we be able to come into
contact with the elemental forces from the lowest,
perhaps, such as the gnome who has charge of the
green things in the garden, to the highest of his
Ray who is the earth Deva in the ethereal realms
—or shall we say a Master of the ethereal realms—
who would direct the formation of the Earth itself.
It is an earth Deva, a fire Deva, a wind Deva or a
water Deva, each at the head of his Ray, who causes
earthquakes, fires and explosions, mighty storms
and floods.   They act under the direction of the
planetary Lords to help humanity pay off the pain
of old Karma or create new, as the case may be.
Therefore, you must remember, that acording to
your element you can come into touch with one of
these Beings, and if your force is strong enough, if
your desire is pure enough, you have the power,
when working through your Ray in the thought
kingdom, to reach these Great Beings of the elements and prevent fire and flood, storm and earth-
quake.

Especially, too, must you remember that the
Devas, being as it were non-human, have not the
same reasoning power as the Lords of the elements.
They stand half-way between the human and the
angel, and as they make closer contact with man,

he, receiving of their grace and beauty and giving them in return gratitude and love and high thought, creates for them a step nearer the God-head. And so man, although to-day degraded in many respects by giving way to the lower passions, is yet a God in the making, and the God part of him is that which awakens and desires union with God. In the God side of him he is given the power in meditation to contact the unseen realms of the ethereal worlds that he may use all its powers to bring him nearer to God.

People who greatly love their gardens are very often able to come into touch with a Deva on the Ray of the earth elements; whilst those who greatly love the sea come into touch with a Deva of the water elements. Those who greatly love trees, as they make their minds receptive, will hear a peculiar, sighing, softly humming sound. I would remind one of you here that you heard a strange humming sound in your garden. By love of your garden you have made contact with a Deva, and if I remember rightly your garden had never been so profuse in giving you of the fruits of your labours.

As you give out love and understanding to these Beings, and talk to them and reach them on the mind plane, quickly will they manifest to you. Very often they attend your séances, bringing flowers as apports. You have thought perhaps that this is the work of a disembodied spirit, but these beings act as the servants of disembodied spirits, bringing through to you love tokens. It is the Devas of the earth element, using a lower and lower vibration until it reaches down to the gnomes, that brings into manifestation from their kingdom the things you treasure of the earth. It is the Devas of the wind that bring you cool and hot breezes in your séance room, and the Devas of water that bring you a condition which is so often expressed in the words : " I feel as though I were up to my knees in water." These Beings of the elemental kingdoms become then the workers of phenomena, and as you realize that they are the workers of phenomena and the servants of your beloved, so do you, by your love and attention, enable them to manifest more clearly.

I do hope that I have made clear the work that is done by the inhabitants of the Devic Kingdoms, because I want you to understand that Devic Initiation can be a part of your training. Let the Devic Kingdoms and the elemental kingdoms know that you are aspiring to gain knowledge from their kingdoms for the upliftment of humanity, and for the glory of God; then quickly do they draw near, telling you the secrets of their kingdoms and initiating you that you may be known amongst all the kingdoms of the elemental planes as one who has attained to Mastership along these lines.

When once you have entered into contact with these kingdoms you understand the speech of animals. You understand what is necessary for the nourishment of the things that grow in the earth.

You can still the waters and the storm. I have only
to mention two great souls who had undertaken
Devic Initiation—St. Francis of Assisi, and Jesus
of Nazareth. Jesus of Nazareth had taken Initiation in the Devic kingdom of the water elements.
Thus He was able to walk upon the water; thus
He was able to perform miracles with loaves and
fishes; thus He was able to cast out the evil spirits
from the swine, who, you are told, went into the
water; because He called upon those Beings of
the water elements to help Him. In that way He
used His knowledge of the water elements for the
cleansing and the healing of humanity. And as
you, finding out in your own Horoscope your
strongest element, ally yourself with that strong
element and call or respond to the call of your particular Deva, you draw them near to you and they
teach you of all that belongs to their realm. You
then receive your Initiation and become a Master
on that Ray. You have seen people who are able
to hold fire without being burnt. They are those
who have been initiated into the element of fire,
and they have their Deva, or perhaps they would
say their Angel, who protects them by right of their
initiatory powers. All who perform feats of this
kind, you may be sure, have come into contact
with the Lords of the Elements of the Ethereal
Realms pertaining to one or more of the elemental
kingdoms.

It is such a vast subject that I find it difficult to
portray to you these different kingdoms in their

different stages, but when you begin to realize how many dimensions there are and how many senses you have that you can unfold, life becomes more interesting, and you are less likely to fall down and worship a Deva if you suddenly become clair-voyant and see him or her as the most celestial, ' radiant and wonderful being.

The Devas are the Gods spoken of so often by the old races. They regarded them as Gods of their own element, and different from the Archi-tect of the Universe or the Father in Heaven; and they realized, especially in Egypt, that when the mummy was put into the tomb, according to the departed one's Horoscope having a predominance of the fiery, watery, airy or earthly element, so was the ritual performed over him in order that a Deva from his most important element should be the guardian of the tomb. When you realize this you will understand why disaster sometimes follows the violation of a tomb. If the tomb was opened with the right word of power no harm would fol-low, but, if this procedure is not understood the rights of the guardian of the tomb may be vio-lated and disaster must follow, because the Deva finds that someone has interfered with his or her office, and having been bound by ritual or promise or bound by power, to be the guardian of that place, he knows that he must guard it until he is released.

Imagine, for instance, a great and mighty Deva of the earth element being called by ceremony and ritual to guard the tomb of a departed one who understood his ways and had tried to help him. you will understand that he would guard it by every power he had; therefore did any one try to violate that tomb, he would use all the forces at his command, and perhaps bring about a fall of masonry or a fall of earth, and disaster would follow. You could hardly blame a non-evil, non-human, non-thinking force, any more than you could blame a faithful dog you had set to guard an article of clothing, if some one coming to steal that article of clothing were bitten.

These non-human Devas are Beings of great beauty. They have the power to bring you perfumes and to protect you when in danger. They are, as it were, the servants or astral protectors of your own particular element. They are very beautiful in appearance. I do not know if it is possible for me to give you more than a faint idea of their appearance. The face is usually very clear-cut and sharp-featured. The forehead high and the cheekbones rather prominent but narrowing off here to almost a triangular shape. They have eyes that slant a little. The ears are rather long and pointed, such as you have often seen in the little demons of your fairy tales, and coming long to the lobe are pointed at the top. The hair is fair with those belonging to air and fire, but with the earth gnomes it is usually dark; it grows high from the forehead, seeming to stand more like a frame around the head, making a sort of halo. They have not bodies

as you understand bodies in the human sense.
They are composed of ethereal matter and only take
form, rather as flimsy drapery; at least that is the
best description I can think of. You have seen the
wing of the firefly—it is very transparent and gos-
samer-like, and it has beautiful and irridescent colouring. Sometimes when these Beings meet a
human who acknowledges their closeness, you will
see them glow with beautiful rose and flame like
the heart of the opal. At other times when they
have been attracted to a garden by some one who
loves nature, they will take on the most gorgeous
colourings of blues, mauves and greens. The
Devas that reside upon the hill-tops, you will find
clothed in glowing colours of pearly-white, and
also pale golden, amethyst and mauves. Those
who are deep in the forest you will find clothed
in the palest green, like the tender shoots of
young trees. You will find that the greens deepen
into blues and they take on the most lovely shades
of colour. If you can imagine this colouring with
a light behind it making it glow, it is very beautiful.

Do try, each one of you, to come into touch
with the Devic kingdom. It is thrilling for you to
hear for the first time that humming sound which
is like nothing on earth. Perhaps the sound of a
thousand bees humming in the distance is the
nearest you have to it and yet it is so close to you,
and when you hear that sound try to raise your
consciousness on to the higher planes, so are you

able to come into touch with them, and they will reward you with loving service. Never will you find yourselves at a disadvantage, but in their presence your thoughts must always be pure and full of loving kindness, coupled with a desire to serve others, because, whilst fire can warm it can also burn; and likewise, whilst earth is good and the smell is pleasant it also can at times become swampy and suck you down into the mud. Wind can fan you with gentle breezes, but it can also become a destroying hurricane, and you will realize that even in the water there can be the quiet, calm bay, or the sea flashing in wild fury and waves beating high. In these you in your nature have the power to bring out all that is beautiful; but if they fail to see good desires in your heart, they will turn to all that is destructive in their nature, because they will be the reflectors of your emotions, and you should not blame them, as many mediums do. Often people who have sat with mediums, have drawn all unwittingly one of these Beings from the Devic kingdom and it has acted as their guide. And then, because of something low or evil in their own nature, they declare that their guide has let them down. Every developing psychic should try to find out whether he or she is being controlled or advised by a discarnate human or by one belonging to the elemental kingdoms. It is one of the dangers of psychism that too little is known about this subject, and so you will ask—How are we to know? If you develop with one who has true clairvoyant sight, and wisdom enough to tell the difference between spirits who have been clothed in matter and spirits who are only clothed in etherea, then you cannot go wrong, but remember, according to your own nature you will attract to you, either the good, the wise and the beautiful, or the foolish and destructive.

QUESTIONS

Q. Does a Deva ever take a human incarnation?

A. Very rarely, but many highly evolved human beings often take a Devic Initiation.

Q. I-Em-Hotep, is the Master Serapis still working with the Devas?

A. He has taken a Devic Initiation that He may be able to tell us more about the way they live, their thought, their language, and how we can better use the powers that they are willing to mingle with our own.

Q. Is the humming sound of which you spoke made by the Devas of all the four elements?

A. They all make this peculiar humming sound. The earth elemental makes rather a deeper sound than the air elemental, but it is all of a peculiar humming quality. With the rediscovery to-day of what you term " wireless," it may be possible with the advance of science that new discoveries will be made which will help you to understand, as we on this side understand, that every flower has its own particular note. When your consciousness is raised and you walk in your garden, the harmony of the various sounds given out by the flowers is something that is very beautiful. Great musicians have sometimes received their inspiration in this way, otherwise, how do you suppose music like the Dance of the Gnomes or the Fire Spirits could have been composed?

Q. Is it possible to take Devic Initiation and not be aware of it?

A. No, my friend, I have often said that it is impossible to take any Initiation without being aware of it. People who tell you that they are in touch with various Masters and have taken Initiation on the Inner Planes, are nearly all fools self-deluded. Can you imagine, my friend, a soul being in daily contact with its Masters and receiving the wisdom of the Gods —can you conceive of that soul being proud, selfish and mean? Can you conceive of that soul hurting another in any way whatsoever? Your answer must surely be " No "; and unless the life shows by its beauty, its humility, its unselfishness, its desire to serve others, then it has not received an Initiation.

Q. With which group did St. Francis of Assisi take his Initiation?

A. He took his Initiation both with air and earth.

Q. You said that the earth Devas gave a deeper note than the Air Devas. Is the note of the air Devas like a thin, reedy sound?

A. It is almost like the note E of a violin. In the G string of a violin you have the note of the Earth elemental. In the D string you have the Water, in the A string the Fire, and in the E string the Air. Do not confuse these notes with the Rays of the elemental; the notes I have given you refer to the sound only.

Q. Are the sounds only heard in gardens which we ourselves have cultivated with love, or does one hear them in the fields?

A. One hears them in gardens and fields.

Q. I-Em-Hotep, when you have a group of people who are singing in a special key, do they attract special Devas to the place where they sing?

A. If you have mass singing, you would only attract the Devas of sound, but if there were in that choir one individual whose heart was singing to a Devic Being, then it would attract that one.

Q. What governs the migrations of birds?

A. It is the will of the air Devas guiding them like a shepherd his sheep. In a similar way an earth Deva can help an animal that is lost to find its way home.

Q. I have had it explained to me that an animal will find its way home under the direction of the group mind?

A. According to your grade or school or Ray, so must the same teaching be clothed in different

K

words; it matters not whether you call it a Deva or a Group Mind. I am trying to give you a more personal explanation concerning the inhabitants of the Devic Kingdom, so that you, as you come into touch with these forces, may not be misled into thinking that you are touching a spirit on a particular plane, when in reality you may be touching, perhaps, one who is on a Ray of the elemental kingdom, one who is serving you, who is governing you, who is guiding you; but you must not be dismayed when you are in contact with a worker on a Devic Ray, if your messages are sometimes unreliable.

Q. Are animals conscious of the Devic world?

A. A dog will be excited and roll about quite happily if a Deva of the elemental kingdom is nigh, but becomes frightened at the approach of a disembodied spirit. For that reason, in days of old, we had animals about the Temple.

Q. When a human being takes a Devic Initiation does he lead a dual life, human and Devic?

A. When human beings take a Devic Initiation they have power over that particular element of which they are on the Ray. The power to bring into manifestation from another dimension shows that there is power on that particular Ray. As I explained to you, the one who can take fire and not be burned would have taken an Initiation on the Ray of the Fire Deva. This is done by most occultists who are studying the other side of life. These, apart from coming into communication with discarnate humans, come into touch with the various inhabitants of the other realms, and they learn from them the laws of power controlling the different elements of earth, air, fire, and water; and perhaps become a materializing medium or an apport medium or one who produces light or handles fire or one who can walk on water. You see they have power over an element.

Q. I-Em-Hotep, did I understand you to say that the Devas who produce floods and the eruption of volcanoes and earthquakes, are working under the Planetary Lords, and that we, if we have sufficient force, have power to influence the Devas and prevent these things?

A. That is so, my daughter. As people realize their inherent, God-given powers, and have purity of aspiration, they become a force for good, and send it out. It is picked up by the Planetary Lords. This is an example of the wise man ruling the stars, or in other words you are contacting the Karma of the planet, and thus by the power of your thought transmuting or extending the time for another cycle. Your great Saviours of the World, the Lords of Karma, continue with their work, but, from time to time, a great soul volunteers to come into incarnation and lift some of the Karma of the world, thus disaster is stayed by the power of His thought. This happened time after time

and is one of the meanings of the word cruci-
fixion, which in some cases you make liken to
a manifestation of the Christ Force seeking to
work through a body, the owner which had
volunteered to give up his personality that the
power might work through him for the purpose
of preventing, shall we say, a flood or a fire.
As you know, from time to time, Great Ones
of this type give up for the time being their own
evolution that they may make sacrifices for
you.   These Great Ones incarnate and have
been used by the Christ of the Ages, or the
Cosmic Christ, or the only Son of God, which-
ever way you like to put it.

Q. Does the sacrifice made by these Saviours effect
a permanent reduction in world Karma?

A. No, not for all time.   Their sacrifice, however,
might stem the destruction of a large city, or
again if you go back to the great floods of
Atlantis, the great Being of the Sun who offered
himself as a sacrifice in that day was able to
stem the floods over a long period of time.
There were three minor floods before the final
submerging of Atlantis, so that in between
times, many hundreds of years, gave the people time to repent.

Q. Must this destruction come eventually?

A. No, my daughter, because I am sure there are
always great souls who are willing to sacrifice
themselves for the good of humanity, and
whilst the Christ force can find a vehicle

through which to manifest, the world will be saved.

Q. Would the Devas who take on human form come to learn a special lesson?

A. No, they might be drawn by great love to seek contact with humans. They might seek to enter into incarnation with the idea of helping. If you take Anna Kingsford, she was one who belonged to the Devic kingdom and entered into human Initiation that she might do her work, and surely one can only say that the world was considerably the brighter, the happier and the better for her short visit. If you study some of her teaching and apply it in the light that she is talking of the kingdoms of her own element, it will become more illuminating.

Q. Which was her element, I-Em-Hotep?

A. Her element was fire, but I am speaking of the elemental kingdom.

Q. Then are the Devas different from the elementals inasmuch as they have souls?

A. They have not soul in the sense that you understand souls, but if you can imagine the perfection of a Master in comparison with yourselves, then you will understand the difference between a Deva and an elemental. When I speak of the elemental kingdom I am speaking of fire, earth, air and water; but when I speak of a Deva I am speaking of what you might term of God of a Ray, the head of a Ray, as differing from a gnome or a salamander.

Q. Surely there was a soul in Anna Kingsford?

A. Not a soul as you understand it. When one takes on human form one must have an astral sheath. If you look upon a soul as something that is different, of what use to save the soul, because it is only the vehicle of the spirit. Therefore the Deva, being divested of spirit as you understand it, has no need for the vehicle. It will have an astral sheath but no soul.

Q. Is the Deva representative of another aspect of Deity?

A. Naturally, it is representative of the creative side, the form side. Man has to do with the mind side.

Q. You spoke about the animals you had in your Temples. Could you give us further details?

A. On the roof of our Temples it was customary for us to hold seances or sittings as you call them to-day, and we kept within the Temple certain animals which we called sacred and which were set apart. These animals were kept as clean as possible in their living and habits and only mixed with others of their kind. They were, however, allowed to wander about and when outside a circle would give indications as to whether the visitor from the spirit world was of the ethereal realms. If, however, the visitor was a discarnate human, then the cat, which was the animal we mostly preferred, would purr and be very joyous, but if the visitor came from the ethereal realm or was one of another element, then the cat would become disturbed and arch its back and raise its hair. A dog, on the other hand, would welcome an elemental or an inhabitant of the elemental kingdoms, but was afraid of the discarnate human. They were opposite in their ways of expressing fear or joy.

Q. I was thinking more of the way in which animals were represented in the Temples?

A. In my own Temple we had white cats, because originally we took up the healing of the eyes, and we considered that the Goddess Isis, representing the Moon, was helpful to us in the healing of eyes, and so to her, the white cat; and we trained them from kittens to come no further than the outer ring of the circle. Never did they enter, but through their breeding and environment, they became very sensitive. We, as you do to-day, held sittings when we wanted to come into touch with our beloved who had departed from this earthly plane, and we too were liable to deception, even as you, and it was our cats who indicated to us whether there was an intruder. When we sat to learn ritual or magic belonging to any one planet, or for any one ceremony, then they also indicated to us that the elementals of those planets were there, and so very often in our researches, with the help of animals, we were able to check up, and that is how Egypt has become renowned, even after it had fallen into decay, as the land of mysteries and magic, because much time was spent in research, and all the world came to my beloved Egypt for instruction in the Mysteries, because in our Temples no pains were spared in research work. It might interest you to know that the dog was always sacred to Sirius, and other animals to various planets. In time they became, as it were, the sacred animals of the town or Temple where a particular aspect of God was worshipped.

Q. Have animals a sense of right and wrong?

A. It is not until you begin to educate your animals that they have a sense of right and wrong. If you take a dog, for instance, and you are very patient with it, and teach it, you would be able to observe how many words it understood. If you do not teach it words and what they mean, then it will not be obedient.

Q. In the evolution of the elemental kingdom, do the gnomes and the other elementals evolve up to the Deva?

A. Certainly, but they very seldom enter into human incarnation. One could not say never, because under the direction of the Architect of the Universe, all things are possible.

Q. When they evolve into the higher Angel kingdom, do they ultimately become Masters in the sense that humans evolve?

A. Yes, and then they pass through the higher elements. I have only spoken to you of four.

I cannot yet speak to you of the higher ethereal kingdoms which it is also possible for them to inhabit. As I told you in the beginning, I can only just lightly pass over this subject. It is a life study in itself.

Q. Do the two kingdoms always remain parallel? Do they ever blend the mind with the form?

A. It is impossible for a Deva to blend its mind with the human except in an inspirational sense. It is only under exceptional circumstances that one on a Devic Ray will take incarnations on Earth, and that for a very special purpose. Many advanced souls on Earth go into the Devic Kingdom that they may absorb knowledge of that kingdom, so that on returning to Earth, they can teach those who are ready.

Q. Do the Devas have their allotted span, as our physical bodies have?

A. They do not understand age, they do not understand mankind, they are not held by matter. The divine life flows through them.

PRAYER

Oh Thou who art all Light! Thou who didst breathe us forth, we seek to return to Thee laden with experience, that we may be the better instruments for the proving of Thy Word.

Oh Thou our Mother, who hast enriched us in Thy wisdom since the ages began, Thou knowest how weary and worn we are. Give us Thy rest.

Oh Thou our Father, all-wise, all-loving, sending us from age to age to take incarnation that we may return to Thee laden with experience, help us to understand Thy laws, and these Thy children, make their minds receptive that they may be filled with the holy desires of oneness with Thee. Thou who hast given them life, Thou who hast given them their personalities, give unto each one of them that which will the best fit them for Thy service. Help them on the homeward way with loving companionship. Help them with Thy peace, help them with Thy joy, that though the way be hard, though the way be sometimes sad and they seem misunderstood, yet give to them the knowledge that they have incarnated to continue Thy work, and thus help them with peace and joy to be pilgrims on the homeward way. Cover them with Thy cloak that they may be strengthened; give them Thy heavenly food that they be not hungry; cleanse them with Thy heavenly fire, and oh, divine Mother, let the waters of wisdom gush forth from Thy eternal source of life, that they may not be athirst.

Gather us, Thy children, incarnate and discarnate, gather us in one as one, and join us ever closer together in the bonds of love that is Thy Self. Amen.

STELLAR INITIATION

To-NIGHT my teaching may appear somewhat strange, because in speaking of Stellar or Star Initiations I must use simple language, so that those who have little understanding of this teaching may get some glimmerings of the vast truth that lies behind these statements of mine. Those of you who have not the scientific type of mind, and those who are touching this teaching for the first time will find it difficult to comprehend, but in every Age the Truth must come, and those who bring Truth through for the first time have to be the butt of many accusations brought by the ignorant. And so to-night I go a little deeper into the subjects I have been endeavouring to teach you.

Throughout these talks I have been trying to instruct you as to why you are here, from whence you came and whither you are going. I have tried to take your minds above and out beyond the spiritual spheres that surround the Earth. Perhaps, to make it clearer, I may borrow for my example something that you can all study for yourselves, and that is the atom and its composition. Try to imagine the nucleous, the protons, the electrons which make the atom and you will get some comprehensive idea of the solar system and begin to understand how very small a spot the Earth is in this vast field of ether that contains many solar systems. You will also begin to realize that your Earth with its four Moons* is, as it were, a classroom or a reformatory; I think that reformatory is perhaps the better word, because the Earth is the school in which man must gain experience. All other planets have a higher state of being; they are more spiritualized, more etherealized and more beautiful. Each one of you is atttached in one form or another to a planet, and the Rays from that planet are able to reach the Earth, penetrating its field or aura, which is known as the signs of the Zodiac. Thus each one of you, as you come under your own particular sign, will begin to realize that you must not limit your understanding to this physical plane and the spirit plane surrounding it. You have to go beyond the Earth's aura.

When the Eye in each one of you streamed forth from the Great Creator in order to enter into this Solar System, it took time to make the journeys. The memory of these journeys in their totality gives you an expansion of the I-am consciousness and makes you realize that you had a beginning somewhere, that you are something beyond matter. The teaching of all Great Teachers stresses the importance of a person coming into at-one-ment with the Father in Heaven. The Father in Heaven of each individual is the ruler of his planet, and by the ruler of his planet, in this instance, I am referring

* Three of which are invisible.—Ed.

to the planet ruling the rising sign. And you, a spirit, a part of God enclosed in matter, receiving the warmth of the Solar rays, receiving the inspiration of the human race, are incarnate in matter in order that you may gain the experience of a particular sign of the Zodiac and come under the influence of a particular planetary Lord.

You have incarnated in matter so that you may learn to come into touch with the Father in Heaven, and when you have grown to where you have overcome all the lower potentialities of your sign and are vibrating to its higher degrees of your sign, you are then merged into the God-consciousness, or the consciousness of the Father in Heaven; because for the soul to come into touch with the God-consciousness, to have the realization of the Father in Heaven, is to become perfect in its manifestation of that particular sign of the Zodiac. And so we say that when man has perfected himself in gaining experience in his particular sign, that he has undertaken a Stellar Initiation. He then becomes a brother of the six-pointed star; he is no longer the five-pointed star; but becomes one with his Lord and Master, whether it be of Mars, Uranus, Venus, or some other planet, according to his ascendant.

You all know how dual you are in nature; you are all aware of the good and bad impulses; you know that there comes a force that sometimes drives you against your higher desire as a leaf is blown along a path, and you are filled at times with envy; you are filled at times with the desire to hurt, and all the things that belong to the lower personality seem to rise up, and the Higher Light is hidden. Now in taking our Stellar Initiation, if we take it with knowledge, we are able to overcome those lower desires to a greater degree. When we feel an inrush of anger we are able to transmute and subdue it, and if we feel anger against a person, with knowledge, we are able to transmute the red of anger into the rose of love. Sometimes when we feel envy or jealousy of another we are able to transmute that into a higher feeling of brotherhood or helpfulness, and as we each try to overcome the innate faults that belong to the lower personality, then we are truly coming into at-one-ment with the Father in Heaven, responding to the Higher Stellar vibrations and filling our auras with beautiful and more opalescent shades of colouring to an extent that enables the Stellar Rays to penetrate.

And what are the outward signs that we are attaining? The outward signs of attainment unto Stellar Initiation are the peace and the poise that comes from within when one is at peace with God. Your surroundings, because you are emanating stronger forces of peace and love, become filled with an aura of peace, and you find that others are glad to come and bask in the sunshine of your presence. because you are emanating peace and harmony and you are able, as you grow, to emanate more and more the strength that comes through contact with your Father in Heaven. Every soul, as it strives with knowledge to make the higher contacts, realizes that it passes, while yet incarnate, through the various spheres of spirit because the spiritual planes and the spiritual inhabitants of those planes, rise, as you do, according to their higher aspirations. To assume that a soul who has passed over rests for ever in a state of inertia and inactivity is not in accordance with truth, because a soul only discards the more material form, leaving the mind to go on aspiring age after age, and some of your friends in the spirit world may come back and tell you that they are making progress, inasmuch as they are touching their Father in Heaven. Many of you may not like this idea, but whether you like it or not it is the truth, and the truth you must have.

From time to time your spirit friends may tell you that your type of thought is helping them to progress. It may amaze you to find that you can help them in this way, but, have you ever considered why you are linked with those who have passed on? You think sometimes it is only the tie of love, but it is something very much more, because in a family or community there is a certain harmony or link in all their Horoscopes, and so you will find, for instance, that a whole family may have a predominance of fire; or again, that perhaps six out of seven of a family may have the sign of Scorpio rising and the one remaining Taurus rising. Although perhaps born in different months and years, they have incarnated in that family that they may help each other in the experience that they have come to gain ; and it is the Sun shining, as it were, through different coloured glasses for each one, colouring the personality and helping each of them to grow and expand and see the many different sides to the one sign, thereby gaining experience and so helping each other. It is well-known that the different degrees of the signs make a great difference to the personality ; therefore, each one must find out the individual sign, the individual degree, and work for its perfection. And as you are working towards this perfection you are influenced and, in a sense, accompanied by the Lord of your particular Planet, who on the various planes becomes your guide and Guardian Angel. In this way each Planetary Lord acts as the Servant or Messenger of God the Father.

The road to at-one-ment may be likened to a ladder of many steps, up which a soul must climb according to its vision and understanding. The nature of this climb may be demonstrated if we consider the sign of Scorpio. I take this sign because it is regarded by some Astrologers as one of the most malefic. Take a lower Scorpio personality and we have one who is filled with low cunning, who is secretive and jealous, who is underhand and mean and given to stabbing people in the back. Now you can imagine a soul incarnating with the sign of Scorpio rising, but placed in an environment that is not conducive to the throwing off of the lower aspects of that sign, and yet karmically the Sun Ray may be one of purity, and the spirit incarnating with all those binding conditions is ever striving by the experience gained to break free. Its Guardian Angel, seeing the strivings, sometimes leads such a soul to where it can become awakened to its spiritual possibilities, and so in the course of time we find the higher aspects of the Scorpio nature beginning to exhibit themselves, and jealousy is converted into a desire to help others. We find that cunning is converted into intellect, that all those lower aspects have become things of beauty, and so we no longer have the symbolism of that which creeps and crawls upon the ground, but the symbolism of the golden eagle that unfolds its wings and flies towards the Sun. It is the lower part of the Scorpio nature, redeemed and cleansed, and released from the prison house of the lower personality, that rises on wings of speed and strength to join its Father in Heaven.

With every sign you have the two aspects, and as you strive day after day to bring out all that is pure and good in your nature, as you strive to create harmony and brotherhood; as you strive to stamp out all that is petty and mean, so you are taking your Stellar Initiation. You are helped by your Solar and Lunar map, you are aided by your Guardian Angel, and in time you can say as the Master Jesus said: "I and My Father are One." You must remember that the Master Jesus too, overcame all that belonged to the lower personality, and when He realised that it was not within Him any longer to feel scorn or irritation, or even to feel

L

hurt at those who reproached Him and gave Him unbrotherly words, then He could truly say : "I and my Father are One." And each one of you here has the same power to reach your Father in Heaven, who is the Lord of your Star. And as you feel the inflow of love and strength, as you learn your note of music, as you learn to meditate upon your colour, as you hold your jewel in your hand, then you are making a contact on the physical plane that sends its echoes throughout all the ether until it touches those with whom you are linked in the planet that perhaps you cannot see.

Those of you who have been taught that this world is the beginning and end of everything, or have considered Earth and Heaven in the more or less conventional way, will find it is difficult to think of them as just one tiny unit on a string of many pearls. As you study the things that I am trying to bring through to you, I would have you remember that only a few hundred years ago you were unaware that your world was spherical in form and that other civilizations and other continents had existed and passed away. But, as you open your minds now and become receptive, so can more and more of the power of the other world become clearer to your understanding.

QUESTIONS

Q. You say that each sign is ruled by a Planet and each Planet ruled by its Lord. Does that mean that there are twelve Fathers in Heaven?

A. Yes, my child.

Q. Am I right in thinking of God and the Master Jesus as our Father in Heaven?

A. Think of Jesus as the Lord of Neptune. He is the Christ of the Piscean Ray, therefore He is the Lord of Neptune.

Q. When we are praying in the words of the Master Jesus: "Our Father which art in Heaven," are we praying to different Fathers?

A. You are not using the prayer of Jesus in the form that He gave it when you say: "Our Father who art in Heaven," but if you say "Our Father who art in Heaven . . ." with the consciousness that you are seeking to touch your Planetary Lord, then your prayer is far more potent than praying in a parrot-like manner. I find as I touch you that your minds are fixed; you accept a man-made religion that is but a few hundred years old like a child with a toy that it likes; all your attention is focussed upon it and you look neither to right nor to left. The more you study and the more you grow, the clearer becomes your vision.

Q. You spoke of different grades of Angels, from the personal to the Regent of a Planet. Could you tell me if all those Angels may be regarded as Guardian Angels?

A. When I spoke of them as going from the personality upwards, I had in mind your Masters who are incarnate and who are also come upon your Ray. Your signs draw you to your Master's notice and they receive instructions regarding you from those who are still higher in grade in the other Worlds. You contact your Guides, Masters and Guardian through your own sign.

Q. I have not become used to the idea that our prayers do not go straight to God, straight to the Architect of the Universe?

A. My daughter, if you pray to the Architect of the Universe, then truly you are praying to the Great God of all, His name is spoken in the Great Silence and is not known to man; therefore man has created a word and so he has called it in your tongue—God. When you pray to God the Father you are speaking to the God of this Solar System. When you pray to your Father in Heaven you are praying to your Planetary Father or Lord of your rising sign. I suggest that you pray to the Great Architect of the Universe. No one comes between you and Him-Her.

Q. Are we under the direction of the Father of a Planet for that one incarnation only?

A. If you have not learned the lesson of a sign in one incarnation, you reincarnate, perhaps, many times again in the same sign, perhaps in different degrees, but you return time after time until you have learnt the lesson. Each time perhaps a little further on the upward grade.

Q. Then does that mean that if you are born in the early degrees of the Zodiac, that you have only incarnated a few times?

A. No, no, you may have made the round many times, but until you have learnt all the experience of the sign you will come back again in that sign in different periods.

Q. I gather that a knowledge of the degrees and their meanings would help one to understand the kind of lesson to be learnt. In Cancer there are thirty degrees; would each of these degrees give different types of experience?

A. The different degrees of a sign are the method of approach and the environment in which the soul has to learn the same lesson. Cancerians have the same lesson to learn, the overcoming and the purifying of the emotions, the overcoming of selfishness; and it may be that with different degrees of Cancer rising, so the environment, the appearance and the grade of social life would alter, according to the experience of the soul already gained.

Q. But the supreme lesson to be attained would be the same for all the degrees, I suppose. The overcoming of those emotions you have enumerated?

A. Naturally. Certain degrees of Cancer may give, perhaps, an extraordinary amount of mother-love. The mother would be selfish in her love, she would be tenacious, too, in her love, and would give way to emotional stress and storm if one encroached upon what she considered should be her domain regarding her

child. In the case of a man, he might be pos-
sessive of his wife, his all as it were. It may
be that he would have a great love of the home
that had been in his family for generations,
and in both cases the lesson would be to let go.

Q. You have likened the Earth to a Reformatory.
Are we very wayward children?

A. I would not call you wayward children because
many of you have incarnated of your own free-
will; many of you have incarnated out of love
or out of a desire to serve. You must remember
that in a Reformatory School there are many
grades.

Q. You say that we transmute anger. Is there
such a thing as a righteous anger?

A. Well, I should say there is perhaps a legitimate
anger, but it is a subtle distinction. One may
feel annoyance, possibly, but in taking the
large view of things one realizes that nothing is
worth anger, it is a waste of energy. To affirm
continually that you will not give way to anger
is helpful.

Q. I-Em-Hotep, when you spoke of criticism being
a fault to be overcome by Virgo people, it is
very difficult to know exactly where to draw the
line, because if we don't criticise we make such
mistakes. We must to a certain extent judge
the actions of others to take our proper place
in the world.

A. My daughter, you have made a very fine distinction. To judge the actions of others and

to keep them within the mind is not harm-criticism.   Virgos in an undeveloped state
are fault finding and critical of others and
intensely irritated at the actions of others, but
there is no finer sign in the whole of the Zodiac
when it comes to judging impartially and impersonally, without giving expression to the
views so that no harm is thereby done to the
one judged or shall we say criticised.   It is
the open and the careless criticism that is
harmful.   One has to remember that each individual sets up a standard for himself, and it
becomes natural to criticise another who does
not come up to that standard or does not agree
with it.   That is human nature.

Q. In the case of a Progressed Horoscope, in
course of time you may pass from one sign of
the Zodiac to another; do you then change
your Father in Heaven for that incarnation or
is He co-ruler?

A. He becomes co-ruler.   You are learning the
lesson of another sign.

Q. In a case such as that just mentioned, would
it be advisable for the soul when praying to
pray to the Solar God?

A. My son, if you ask me to whom to pray, I
would say pray to the Architect of the Universe that He gives you the power to feel the
love that He sends through His Ministers to
you.   By meditation and love you come into
touch with your Father in Heaven, but when

you pray, pray to the Architect of the Universe.
I think it would be wise for some of you who
have leasure to study astronomy; it will give
you a wider conception of the Universe.   In
ancient Egypt those who were interested in
Theology were also interested in all the sciences
that pertained to the building of the Cosmos. In
a hundred years time, the things I am speaking of will be taught to the children in your
schools.

Q. I gather, that many of us when out of the body
at night are being taught the laws pertaining to
Astrology?

A. Every one who seeks after knowledge, every
one who seeks to come into at-one-ment with
their guides on the other planes, are taken by
them to the Halls of Learning and there instructed.

Q. Were the Lords of the Planets known to early
man?

A. The Great Lords of the Planets have existed
and been recognized since the beginning of
time. Their names have changed with the different races of mankind.

Q. Is it possible to know them by their original
names?

A. Of course it is, my daughter. There are records
and records and records.

Q. When you speak of Initiation and those seeking the interior way, what Initiation is that,
I-Em-Hotep?

A. There are many forms of Initiation. My talks
to you comprise the teaching of an outer group.
Usually after a period of training, when loyalty
and harmony is proved, a student may be
asked to take part in a ceremony that brings
him into association in a more intimate degree.
He can then say that he has been taken into or
initiated into a particular Order. There are
many Mystery Schools in your world to-day
and each school has its own method of Initiation. Once a Student has been taken into an
Order, he or she makes a promise that cannot
be broken unless the student is prepared to
suffer by the breaking; and the student is
taught the knowledge belonging to that particular Mystery School. Each Mystery School
works upon a particular Ray and under particular guidance. No one school is stronger or
better than another, each school having its part
of the truth, and each one initiated therein making progress as far as he is capable of doing in
this day of life. Does that answer your question?

Q. Partly. I was thinking that when you spoke
to us you mentioned that you yourself would
lead the faithful of your class to Initiation?

A. I did not mean to convey that wholly, my
daughter, because many of you do not belong
to me. Many of you will find your own Mystery
Schools and receive your Initiation therein. I
am afraid that were I to undertake your training

you would not stay with me long, because the Egyptian School is very thorough and brooks no disloyalty.

Q. How *could* any of us be disloyal?

A. Could you not? There are many of you disloyal in this room.

Q. But in anything to do with God it is unthinkable?

A. Oh, to do with God. Many of you may think that I am not to do with God. What then? Always in groups there are mixed conditions, but to balance that we look at the other side and we find those who are filled with love and loyalty, and our heart is warmed and our spirit sings, and it is for the few that are loyal and the few that are seeking, we do the work of the Architect of the Universe. Every group must have its Judas, and every group must have its Peter, and every group its John. It has been so since the beginning of time and methinks it will be until the end of time.

Q. Does the aura indicate the rising sign of a person?

A. No, my son, but I think the colour of the background of your aura would indicate the place or sign of the Moon in the Horoscope. The colour of your aura is modified by the emotions and thoughts you have builded into it since the moment of your birth. It is rather like an opal but varies with the emotions, health and personal conditions, but it plays upon a background of one colour.

Q. Some time ago you gave us a meditation in which we had to visualise the new Moon growing to the full Moon and reflected in the water. Will you now give us another exercise?

A. I cannot do better than revert to the exercise you have mentioned but, with a different symbol. Meditate upon the picture of a Moon hanging low in the sky over a field of ripening corn. First image the Moon as a sickle, then gradually growing larger and brighter and brighter until the whole picture seems to become golden against a background of dark blue. Take three breaths, visualising a line of light to the heart centre, passing from the heart centre, through the lungs, throat and out through the nostrils. This should revivify the heart centre and open some clairvoyant faculty. Practice it like the previous exercise only do it in threes.

PRAYER

Oh Thou who are the Architect of the Universe, we Thy children incarnate and discarnate seek to draw near to Thee. We thank Thee that Thou hast overshadowed us with Thy love. We adore Thee, oh Thou our Creator, and we seek to come into at-one-ment with Thee through our endeavours to cleanse ourselves of all that is left in us of the lower personality.

To these Thy children incarnate give unto them an Angel Watcher, and to us Thy children of spirit, grant fortitude, grant understanding, and grant love to minister unto them.

And we ask Thee oh Thou who art Father and Mother, Thou who art the Author of all worlds, to have patience with our endeavours to fit ourselves for Thy service. Let the Mother side of Thee tenderly heal and bless all hurts of these Thy children, and let the Father side of Thee fill them with courage in all their ways of experience.

Now send down upon them the heavenly food and fire, that Thy peace may be with them always.

Amen.

LUNAR INITIATION

LUNAR INITIATION in this day of life covers a wide field and is of very great importance to man. It takes place when man builds the faculty of remembrance, when he has succeeded in loosening his various bodies, for a Lunar Initiate is one who is able to leave his body in order to travel on the seven planes, record his findings and converse with those he meets thereon.

Naturally the question will arise in your minds : "How should we begin our preparation to enable us to function consciously on the astral planes?" First, I would give you a few words of warning, because I am told that there are to-day many books and many teachers who advocate the opening up of the Psychic or Lunar Centres. The more you understand of magic, of ritual, and of the Inner Mysteries, the more your realize the dangers. People sometimes enter into a psychic condition because they have an awareness of other worlds. They are able to see or sense a little, and naturally they wish to so perfect this gift that it may serve them and their fellows. In the first awakening it is usual to find that people are distressed that their psychic powers are not developed more quickly. In their ignorance, they fail to realize that although they have earned the right to the unfoldment of psychic powers, they have forgotten the key which opens the door and gives them the entry into the spirit world, and the Holy Guardian Angel, who sometimes assumes the form of guide or teacher, is hard put to it to hold the instrument from breaking the psychic vows; because in most surroundings and most circles, unless there is the right mixture of auras, unless there is purity of life and purity of motive, the seeker after Lunar Initiation finds himself entangled in the astral web, and here he begins to meet with those who belong to the elemental kingdoms, mischievous sprites who will frolic and assume many parts, and if our psychic student is of the type that is smug and self-satisfied, and feels that because he has touched the outer edge of the etheric world he is in no need of teaching, he quickly becomes obsessed or a prey to the lower astral enticements, and although these seem for a time to give him perchance the power of prophecy, or the power to perceive a little more, this power may be of short duration, in which case the whole thing is closed down leaving the student in great distress of mind if not actual mental unbalance.

I advise you to remember that we are dealing with Lunar forces. Lunar forces govern the lower mental planes; they govern the psychic body and they govern the astral as well as the material tides in your world; they are also the waters of illusion. When a man realizes his ignorance of the things that can retard or hinder his growth, he begins to be more careful in the choosing of his teacher or school, and he is not dismayed when his teacher begins to cure him of some of the quaint ideas he has regarding himself, because he is taught that love is the law, and that if he would be a Master on the psychic or lunar planes, he must overcome all of the lower personality. His mind must be pure, and by purity of mind I mean that he must not speak against his neighbour, he must be honest and straightforward and pure of living and he must ever strive to serve the Gods. With this aim in view, sitting for his Psychic or Lunar unfoldment, he comes into closer rapport with the Holy Guardian and there is mutual benefit, for the Holy Guardian appointed to man will lead him, as long as he remains pure, along the upward spiral, through the lower to the higher astral planes, to where he can come into touch with those Higher Intelligences, those Masters of Wisdom and those great White Brothers yet incarnate; and here he receives instructions as to how he must guide his life and care for his body; why it is wise to do certain meditation and certain Yogi practices.

Before a student sits in a circle he is instructed that he should partake of what you term the Feast of Remembrance, and if he seeks to tread the Lunar path and to develop on the psychic and astral planes, he should, before any meditation or any sitting in a circle for development, purify his aura, purify his mind, and come into at-one-ment with the particular aspect of God which he worships. I mean in this wise if you are a follower of the Master

Jesus, you will partake of the sacrament that is assigned to Him. If you are a follower of one of the Eastern Schools, you will partake of the Holy Sacrament assigned to that aspect. The partaking of this sacrament is in itself a magical rite, because the student before seeking to loosen the physical from the astral body is cleansing the atoms, cleansing the whole of the cells, is cleansing the mind; he is identifying himself with God : the physical body is cleansed and purified, and is left in the care of those who make around it a sacramental feast. Then, there is no danger of obsession, there is no danger of unbalance, because the student has made his ritual of cleansing, has identified himself with the Godhead, therefore he is one with God in all his atoms and his body is free from all impurities that would attract to itself anything of an obsessing nature, leaving the spirit part free, so that in his circle or place of meditation he can slowly withdraw the spirit from the body and begin to take his instructions on the astral planes.

Astrology, symbolism, colour and sound, although subjects sometimes maligned by the ignorant, are of great use during this stage of growth, and our student, as he takes his sacrament, determines to meditate and touch everything pertaining to Mars, so when thinking of Mars he thinks of the colour red and the symbol and number of Mars, etc. Having prepared himself for his astral journey, everything he meets, whether spirit, elemental or angel, whether colour, star or whatever symbol it may be, should show some quality pertaining to Mars. If the student is in the right vibration he does not expect any astral entity to mislead him with any symbolism of Saturn; for he will begin to understand why the teacher in the earlier stages, whilst teaching Initiation, the Hermetic philosophy and the Hermetic principle of development, lays stress on learning something of symbology, something of the law of the planets, something of number and colour and sound, so that when the student is sent away from the body for his astral journey, the teacher will perhaps have made a link with the student and will say " I have sealed certain symbols; now I release you to go on your journey "; and when the student comes back and relates what he has seen on his Astral journey, the teacher is then able to understand if he has the right astral constitution for certain experiments.

Therefore the student in the course of time can take that same procedure and can make an invocation to the Holy Guardian Angel, we will say of Venus, and then in his astral travels he will expect to come into touch with the Angels of Venus; he will expect to find their symbolism even on the astral plane surrounding this world. And so our Lunar student begins to take his first Initiation on the Astral Plane. He knowswhat he is going to see; he knows that he is well protected in the material consciousness because, he has taken the right protective measures for the material body. As these facts become more widely known you will

M

find in the future that your psychics, and your mediums will be of a much higher order, because they will have the knowledge that first and foremost purity of motive and purity of life is necessary. They will understand that alcohol or smoking in any form, is detrimental to true psychic growth, therefore, they will be sane, balanced people, instead of perhaps neurotic self-seekers. As the student begins to function in the Lunar Consciousness, he will not be caught up in the web of illusion, but will see the clear reflection of the Queen of the Heavens, guiding him on the upward way, bringing to him symbols of plant, mineral, animal, all from the past, so that down the ages he will see the progress he has made; he will see the mistakes he has made and he will, with clarity of mind and integrity of purpose, become stronger in his development and, having once absorbed the beauties of the astral worlds, he will never cease until he can function consciously on the Solar Realm, the highest spiritual plane.

All the great teachers of the past have undertaken this Initiation. Every one who seeks to become an active member of the White Brotherhood must take this Initiation also. It is one of the steps that makes you an Adeptus Practicus. Therefore, do not be dismayed when you feel that some of my talks are unnecessary or some are misleading. I seek to train you, not with promises that you will attain under any circumstances, but I promise that you will attain if there is selflessness of purpose and purity of life and purity of motive. The Holy Guardian Angel attached to each one of you will never open to you the secret of the Inner Realms if it is for selfish ends, but neither must you be dismayed if at times you find the whole of your sensitiveness closed down. Rather learn to come into closer touch with the Holy Guardian; and learn to rely upon Him, knowing, that since you are seeking unfoldment to serve God, all things are working for your good.

If you are in a circle and some part of you rebels, it is wise to leave that school and not blame your fellow students for something that may be within yourself. It is wise in taking your Lunar Initiations, or any Initiations whatsoever, to adhere to one school, because, whilst all schools are good, each school has its own procedure and you cannot mix the grades. You cannot mix the types of meditation or Yoga. Each Master of a Temple is striving to lead you according to the light given to him, according to his understanding of your possibilities. Therefore it is essential that you have faith in your teacher, loyalty to your school and a desire to serve God in purity and selflessness. Remember that you are under the law, and the law of God is love; not a sentimental, lip-serving love, but a heart serving love that loves in spite of the frailty of human nature; that loves the fellow student in spite of the faults of the personality; that is every ready to lend a helping hand and to wash the feet of the wayfarer; and as you strive day after

day, so you will feel yourself begin to radiate, begin to give out an essence that has the radiance of
our Lady of the Moon. Remember the symbolism
of Isis, all the Initiations of Isis, all the Initiations
of the Moon, the Initiations of Hathor and the Initiations of Venus. And if you accept the teaching
or the overshadowing of one of these Great Beings,
so must you learn to identify yourself with them
and trust them; so must you meet them on the
astral planes without wavering. If you, the product
of your age, would take an Initiation on the astral
plane you can invoke Isis in the form of the Virgin
Mary. If you would take the Initiation of Horus
you can invoke the presence or the overshadowing
of Jesus, because Jesus, Mary, Isis, Horus are all
manifestations of the same Great White Light
penetrating through each age, bringing the God-
light to inflame the hearts of men and women.

Always remember that you must choose. You
have freedom of choice and you accept one or the
other as the form with which you will identify
yourself, even as your Master Jesus would say : '' I
and my Father are One,'' so must you, before your
meditation, before your sitting, before your astral
travelling, identify yourself with that Ray of Light
which you have chosen. Having chosen your Ray
of Light, adhere to it until you have received Mastership, until you have reached the highest grade
and are freed from all personalities and come face
to face with your Father in Heaven. Remember
there are many Mystery Schools; there is the cloak

which uses the same symbols, it has but given the Gods different names, and so through all your days of time you are meeting the same force, the same symbolism and the same imaging of the Gods, but having chosen your school you must adhere to it; if you do otherwise you may become confused. Imagine for a moment the type of seeker I always term astral or psychic tramps. There are many such. They tramp from lecture to lecture, from school to school, from circle to circle, and when you meet them year after year apparently having made very little progress, they will tell you with a bright smile that they are Universalists. Now that is a waste of force. Far better had they stayed at one school until they have passed all its grades and were exempt from adherence. If they had done this they could have become teachers and formed groups for themselves, but unless there is loyalty and adherence to the chosen path those who silently wait keep fast hold of the door. You cannot entrust secrets of Initiation to a mind that is nebulous and uncertain and swaying this way and that way, uncertain whether it wants to be on the Ray of the Rosy Cross, or in the Golden Dawn of the Sun, or in the Great White Light of the Spirit; a waverer of this type is truly a man of sorrows with no place to lay his head, because he is restless and moves from place to place. I am speaking quite impersonally here, when I say, and again I say it with knowledge, that those who would tread the more interior way, should choose their Master, choose their School, and adhere to that Master and to that School until they have passed all its grades.

I think, perhaps, that is all I can say to you about Lunar Initiation, because you must remember we are starting from the lower end of the ladder, from earth upwards; we are trying to link ourselves with the Great Angels of the Moon who adopted us in the far past, and who are our Fathers in Heaven. To those of you who are students of Astrology, it is wise to come to an understanding of the place in your natal map of the Moon and the aspects which will guide you as to what school it would be wise for you to study under.

QUESTIONS

Q. How are we to know which school it would be wise for us to join?

A. In these talks, we have left the path of psychism and have been treading more or less the path of occultism, although on the very fringe. In the Great White Brotherhood, there are twelve Rays, twelve Masters working on the Earth Plane, and each of these Masters works through groups that are centralised, and these groups or orders are known as Esoteric Schools or Mystery Schools. When you have decided the line of teaching most suitable to your state of growth, method of approach and ideals, and are willing to adhere to that teaching, then you have to send out a strong thought and your teacher is directed towards you, or you make a contact through a lecture or perhaps a casual meeting with a friend or through the invitation of a friend. Having joined your school and feeling happy therein, go wholeheartedly forward that you may receive wisdom and protection and love from the Master under whose Ray it is proceeding.

Q. Have we made that choice in a previous day of life?

A. You may be told so. If you have made the choice it will show in your Horoscope. In a previous day of life it may have been necesary for you to pass through one school and in this day of life through another, otherwise how can you pass through the twelve Rays in order to become a White Adept?

Q. I-Em-Hotep, is it necessary to take the Psychic Initiation first of all, because in some cases we have been told to avoid all psychic things?

A. No, my daughter, there are different doors for every soul. It is most unwise for some pupils to enter by the psychic door at all. In other cases it is most wise for them to do so. Many students enter through Theosophy, New Thought, Christian Science; each one enters through his own door; no door is more widely open than another, it is the individual who must choose. Naturally if you have a square between Neptune and the Moon it would not be wise to enter through the psychic door. If you feel drawn to a teacher or a school it is wise to take your Horoscope to that teacher and ask if its shows any link with the school. If your teacher is a true teacher, he or she will read the map to you and advise you to which school or Ray it would be best for you to go to for your development. All true teachers are impersonal, realizing that it matters very little whether the student chooses one particular school or another so long as the student advances.

Q. What is the technique of meditation?

A. Everything has its own technique. The technique preceding meditation includes the preparation of environment and place, the right type of breathing and invocations, in fact very much as you would prepare for a ritual. This preparation preceding meditation is a part of the technique of meditation. Is that comprehensive?

Q. Yes, thank you. How do you prepare for a ritual?

A. You select your room. You select your position. You select your symbol, your implements, your incense. Those are the things which lead up to a ritual and which in many ways are similar to the process preceding meditation.

Q. I-Em-Hotep, there must be many people who love God equally as much as we do and they have not been privileged to attend your lectures; they know nothing about ritual; surely they can find God just the same?

A. Certainly they can, my child. No one is left in darkness, every one is led according to his growth. I have told you that some have not left the group mind or group soul, and those who have not left group guidance, study together because they have not the power of discrimination, but only the power of imitation, therefore they do perfectly well in your orthodox religions.

Q. The thought of ritual is to me a little bit frightening. Can one get anywhere without it?

A. Of course one can. I have been most careful not to teach you ritual and until I give you, shall I say, the technique of ritual, then do not attempt it. You must understand that I am an Egyptian and my religion is a ritualistic one, and because I understand my own religion, because I understand all that lies behind its symbolism, it is natural that I should teach you my own method. Were I a Master of your Christian Religion, I should have returned to teach you further the early mysteries of your own religion and churches.

Q. In the course of one of your talks to us you stated that meat was not a legitimate food for man. Now that you are dealing with the subject of Lunar Initiation, I would like to ask if it would be better for a soul to discard meat if he has been in the habit of eating it, and eat nothing we will say but fish and cereals?

A. To eat fish is just as harmful as to eat meat,
but I would say this, my son : it is not wise to
change your diet unless you do it under instruction. If you are seeking to attain some high
grade of Initiation, those who are teaching you
will instruct about the things to leave alone
and the things to take. I do not advocate any
one trying to develop psychically, trying ritualistic practices, trying anything without a
teacher whom they can trust. You must have
a teacher upon the path when you are seeking
the more interior way, unless you have come
into touch with your Holy Guardian Angel and
can hear the voice of the Holy Guardian Angel,

Q. Do you reach the Guardian Angel through the
psychic path or through the mental?

A. You can reach the Guardian Angel, my child.
through pure meditation. You must have some
form of meditation, whether it is prayer or
thought before you can fit yourself to understand what is on the more interior planes. How
do you know, if you have not inner sight, or if
you have not some one with you who has
inner sight, whether you are talking to your
Holy Guardian Angel or some one who is
masquerading? Until you have come into conscious touch with your Holy Guardian Angel
you must have an instructor, no matter what
road you take.

PRAYER

O Thou who art our Father! O Thou who art our Mother! We draw near to Thee in grateful adoration that Thou hast allowed us, Thy children discarnate and Thy children incarnate, to meet together. Let Thy Holy Wisdom flow through each of these that it may bring light into the world. Let Thy peace find an abiding place in each heart here, that it may be a strength that shall grow and a peace that shall prevail over all the Earth, that man may come to a true feeling of brotherhood and love.

Send Thy heavenly food, O divine Mother, for the feeding of these Thy hungry ones. Send Thy cleansing fire, O Thou our Father, for their regeneration, and help them day by day to come into at-one-ment with Thee that they may recognise Thee in all that lives; that they may see Thy face in the face of each other; and may Thy peace abide with them always, Thy love enfold them and Thy strength unhold them in all their ways. Give unto their Holy Guardian Angels strength and power to manifest to them, that they lose not the way that leads them homeward to Thee. Draw near to us that we may feel Thy peace. Amen.

APPENDIX

THE RITUAL KNOWN AS THE WASHING OF THE FEET

MANY of you read in your Bible that Jesus washed the feet of His disciples. To understand the hidden meaning of this, you should know that Jesus taught His disciples a very old Ritual in the form of an exercise based upon three letters. These three letters gave them the symbology behind the washing of the feet and showed that the feet were washed by the Divine Light.

These letters were I, A, O, the mystical name Jesus gave to His Father in Heaven; three great words that make the secret name of God. The " I " symbolizes the Mother aspect—Isis. " A " represents Apophis, the Guardian or Lord of the Underworld, who watches, weighs and tests the soul before it can receive the Light. The " O " symbolizes Osiris the Father aspect. This three-fold aspect of God—Father-Mother-Son, or Light, Darkness and Love—make a Triangle. Is is the bond reaching up towards union with God from the base of the earth.

Those of you who desire to practise this exercise can begin by either standing or lying down with feet turned slightly outwards. Visualize the Master

Jesus. Image a stream of Light coming from His Forehead to your left foot and say " I." From His Heart Centre image another stream of Light coming to your right foot and say " A." Then, image the " O " encircling your heels and a Ray of Light coming from His Solar Plexus. Cencentrate on this and then visualize the Three Streams of Light coming up through your legs and thighs. As you intone the mystical name I, A, O, let this prayer come from your heart : " I seek Thee O Lord, not as I will, but as Thou wilt. May I find Thee and enter into Thine Eternal Love." If you can do this exercise day after day as it should be done, you will find that in about three months time you are growing more healthy in body, clearer in mind, and you will become more serene. The petty trials of life should worry you less and in course of time you will become balanced on all planes of consciousness and grow more like the Master Jesus.

It is quite possible that after you have practised this exercise for about a fortnight, you may feel an intense desire to sleep or you may find your digestive organs exhibit some slight evidence of disturbance; also, you may experience a feeling of great heat. If this happens, do not be alarmed, because the Light of Christ that you have called into being through the sound of the Secret Name— I, A, O—is cleansing your vehicles and bringing you slowly and steadily into Union with God.

Printed in the United States
84875LV00005B/82/A